Phonics and the Teaching of Reading

John M. Hughes

Evans Brothers Limited

Published by Evans Brothers Limited
Montague House, Russell Square, London WC1B 5BX

Printed in Great Britain by Cox & Wyman Ltd., London,
Fakenham and Reading
ISBN 0 237 28529 0   PRA 5218

Contents

Preface

This book is a development of my first book, *Aids to Reading*. As a result of including a few suggestions for the teaching of phonics in *Aids to Reading*, it became apparent that there was a need for a more comprehensive work on this very important aspect of the teaching of reading.

I fully appreciate that when teachers read books and attend courses in order to improve their teaching of reading, they become 'fed up' with all the theorising and almost beg for concrete suggestions to help those of their pupils who are experiencing difficulty.

This book is an attempt to give practical advice to teachers. It contains suggestions for various activities, games and materials related to the teaching of phonic reading. It does not neglect the work that may have been carried out using other methods and approaches, especially the work that has already been done in building up children's basic sight vocabularies, but incorporates these with the many suggestions for phonic teaching.

This book does not purport to present all that a teacher should know about the teaching of phonics. It is intended as a handbook that may serve to encourage teachers to think for themselves and so provide further approaches and innovations. It does, however, make a plea for more systematic and direct teaching of phonic skills. If this book leads to a re-evaluation of existing practices in many classrooms throughout the land, then its aim will have been achieved.

Flexibility, versatility and ingenuity are essential to the successful teaching of reading because of the individual differences in the way in which children learn to read. I do not at any time suggest that one method is superior to another because I have found that any method, practice or approach is likely to work better with some children than with others. I do wish to emphasise, however, that the development of independence in reading depends on acquiring methods of unlocking the pronunciation of words. But, it must be remembered that reading is a process of getting meaning from printed word symbols and is more than just a mechanical process and the making of noises associated with certain symbols.

If, as a result of reading this book, teachers become more aware of the value of phonics in the overall reading programme, then, I believe, they will acquire more confidence in teaching reading and thus assist children in reaching the achievement of independence in reading.

J.M.H. 1972

A Few Important Terms

analysis

the breaking down of a word into its constituent letter sounds.

auditory acuity

sharpness of hearing.

auditory discrimination

the ability to detect differences and similarities in sounds.

auditory memory

the ability to remember a sound which has been perceived.

auditory perception

awareness of a sound sensation.

backwardness

when a child's attainment is well below that of the average child in his class.

blending

bringing together the constituent sounds of a word in order to form the whole word.

cerebral dominance

one side of the body is usually preferred to the other. One area of the brain appears to determine a person's preference.

cross laterality

a lack of established dominance. There may be a different hand dominance from eye dominance, e.g. a right-eyed person who is left handed.

digraphs

two letters which combine to make one sound, e.g. *ch*, *ee*.

diphthongs

two vowels representing one vowel sound.

diacritical marks   marks used to assist the reader in making the correct sounds for symbols.

dyslexia   severe reading disability. Suggested by some to be the result of brain damage. It may be referred to as word blindness.

flash cards   cards containing words or sentences which are briefly exposed to encourage the child in word recognition.

graphemes   letters of our alphabet. Graphemes either singly or in groups represent sound-units ('phonemes') within words.

inversion   a term used when a person sees a letter upside down.

kinaesthetic   using the sense of touch.

look and say   the method of reading using sight words.

left/right orientation   the ability to read from left to right.

mixed methods   the teaching of reading involving a number of methods, e.g. look and say, phonic, and sentence method.

phonemes   sound patterns of spoken language.

phonic method   the teaching of reading when the emphasis is placed upon the sounds of letters.

reading age   a child's reading attainment when compared with the reading standard for the average child.

retardation   a term used when a child's reading attainment falls below his ability.

reversal   reversing a letter or word, e.g. 'on' for 'no', 'was' for 'saw', 'd' for 'b'.

sight vocabulary   the number of words a person can recognise in print.

sight-words   words learned by sight and not by building them up sound by sound.

synthesis   the joining of constituent sounds to form a whole word.

visual acuity   the sharpness of vision.

visual discrimination   the ability to detect differences and similarities in shape, size and colour.

visual memory   the ability to remember a visual image.

visual perception   the ability to be aware of an image which falls on the retina.

word blindness   severe reading disability. May be referred to as dyslexia.

word building   building up a word from its letters or sounds.

word recognition   the ability to recognise a printed word.

1

Why Phonics?

'What kind of language is English? Our system of recording
language is demonstrably phonetic. That is, there is a definite
relation between the sounds of speech and the letter-symbols that
record them. When people say English is not a phonetic language
they really mean that the phonetic system of recording English
speech is erratic and unreliable.

But even though, in English, the correlation between sounds
and symbols does not have a consistent, one-to-one correlation,
there is nonetheless a useable correlation between a sound and
its symbol. To abandon completely the use of this correlation
because of its aberrations and to resort to memorising each word
as if it were an ideograph in a nonphonetic language seems not
only unreasonable but oblivious of the very structure of the
English language.'[1]

Reading holds such a central place in education as a means of
communication in a highly literate society that a brief discussion
of the various methods of teaching reading is of utmost importance in order that we, as teachers, may have a better understanding of the problems involved. Southgate and Roberts[2]
have provided a very comprehensive review of the various
approaches to the teaching of reading.

[1] Stern, C. & Gould, T. S., *Children Discover Reading*, page 8. Harrap, London,
1966.
[2] Southgate, V. & Roberts, G. R., *Reading—Which Approach?* U.L.P., 1970.

The Alphabetic Method

Children learned the names of letters, *ay*, *bee*, *cee* and spelled the names into words, *bee – ay – tee* spells *bat*. We are inclined to be very cynical about teaching in this way, but many children learned to read and to read with reasonable efficiency. The emphasis was on the names and shapes of letters and this no doubt helped the learning of letter sequences, left to right word attack and spelling. It was thought that if children saw letters in their normal order in words, and if they were called out often enough, they would learn to read because the names of many consonants suggest their sounds.

This method must have been difficult and dull consisting as it does of drill rather than meaningful reading. Because the names of many letters are often different from the sounds they represent in words, it must have been difficult for children to appreciate that letters are symbols of certain words and, after all, one letter may stand for several sounds.

The Phonic Method

This approach to the teaching of reading is based on the relationship of sound and letter. During the nineteenth century, the approach began by teaching the child the alphabet. The usual procedure was to draw the child's attention to the form of the printed letter and then tell him the sound it made. Unfortunately, the approach was to associate a strange letter with a meaningless sound. Consonant sounds rarely occur in language without having a vowel sound appended. The sound *ber*, which is the usual way of describing the sound for 'b' (in bat) does not truly illustrate the sound for 'b'. Many consonants are very difficult to pronounce unless a vowel is involved with them. There is a danger that the phonic method may involve meaningless drill and children may concentrate so much on sound that comprehension may be ignored, but there is no reason whatsoever why a phonic method should involve such an approach. In the past, writers of 'beginning reading'

2

books produced much artificial reading material and the vocabulary was limited in both words and meaning.

There has been a realisation during the last twenty years that the differentiation and identification of letter shapes and sounds should not be taught in isolation. For example, in Daniels and Diack's *Royal Road Readers*,[1] the approach involves a phonic word method. The method is based on the idea that material for teaching reading ought to be designed so as to give the child, in as easy manner as possible, insight into the nature of letters. In the *Royal Road Reading Scheme*, the child does not learn the letters in isolation but functioning in words.

The Look and Say or Whole Word Method

This method is based on the conception that children see words as whole-patterns. Children, therefore, memorise the look of words and learn to associate the printed word with meaning. This may be achieved because of the word's overall pattern but more frequently it is because of certain details contained in the printed word. Diack[2] suggests that if a child has no previous information as to which word to expect, he will see particular details before he sees the whole word. This method emphasises the shapes of words and children are not concerned, at first, with letters as such. As many meaningful words as possible are involved, often accompanied by pictorial representations as additional aids. The method may be used to teach the phonically irregular words such as 'are', 'the', 'you'.

There is a danger, however, that individual letters may be overlooked and indiscriminate guessing may result. The main disadvantage of using Look and Say as the sole method of teaching reading is that it does not contain a technique for attempting unfamiliar words and so many children are unable

[1] Daniels, J. C. & Diack, H., *The Royal Road Readers*, Chatto & Windus, London, 1960.
[2] Diack, H., *Reading and the Psychology of Perception*, Roy Palmer, Nottingham, 1961.

to work on their own. There are many children who are unable to learn many whole words at a time and, as a result, reading material has to be produced with strictly limited vocabularies. A great deal of repetition is required and there is a danger that certain materials may involve much mechanical drill and so become as boring as the alphabetic and phonic methods of the past.

The Sentence Method

Here the emphasis is on whole sentences and phrases. This may be regarded as a logical evolution from the Look and Say method. The proponents of this method suggest that even words cannot give much information in themselves, but a short sentence is more meaningful. The theory is that children should learn words in sentences because sentences are the units of thought. Thus children's interests can be utilised and more attractive reading materials can be provided resulting in rapid and fluent reading. But surely it is not true that meaning is to be found only in sentences. Children see many isolated words which have meaning because they imply sentences, e.g. 'school' (Here is the *school*.), 'stop' (You must *stop* here.).

There is a danger that if this method is adopted to the exclusion of others or a 'mixed approach', individual letters and words may be excluded or ignored and this may lead to indiscriminate guessing. Because, once again, there is a necessity for frequent repetition of words, the vocabulary of reading materials may be restricted.

The Kinaesthetic Method

This is a method described very fully by Grace Fernald[1] and has been used by teachers for over forty years, especially when dealing with retarded readers. However there is no reason why it should not be incorporated into a 'mixed method' approach.

[1] Fernald, G. M., *Remedial Techniques in Basic School Subjects*, McGraw Hill, New York, 1943.

4

An experience or interest approach is used. The child is asked to choose a word he thinks is difficult. The teacher writes the word in large writing on a piece of paper, saying each syllable as she writes, and the child traces over the word with his forefinger and, at the same time, pronounces the syllables of the word. The tracing and vocalisation of the word are repeated until the child feels that he can reproduce it without looking at it. When he has written the word on another piece of paper, he may be asked to show his ability to the class by writing the word on the blackboard.

This method of learning new words involves the visual-auditory-tactile-kinaesthetic modes of learning. It must be remembered that the tracing should be with the forefinger. A pencil should not be used because this impedes the child's feel of the word using the tactile and kinaesthetic senses. Eventually, the child produces his own reading material and writes stories about any topics. These will vary in length and any words he does not know are written by the teacher and are learnt by tracing and vocalisation.

My experience over the years in the teaching of reading has convinced me that there are many children failing to read because of their lack of phonic knowledge. Time and time again, I have noticed that even though many children may have acquired fairly large sight vocabularies and continue to assist these sight vocabularies by 'guessing' new words through the use of contextual clues and illustrations, they inevitably encounter many words which are either not recognised by sight or are not read because there may not be contextual or pictorial clues to assist them. It is obviously essential that children must have the necessary tools to unlock many such words.

It is unfortunate that the controversy over the years about the best method of teaching reading has prevented many teachers from appreciating that every method has its place.

For many years, two different methods have each claimed to possess the key to the best method of teaching reading – the Phonic and the Look and Say methods. Many people have advocated one method to the absolute exclusion of the other. There have been charges and countercharges and heated arguments between the two schools of thought. Controlled experiments have been carried out in such a way that claims have been made for a method's relative values. The questions have been – Should the child be taught the letters of the alphabet first and then to learn to sound out words letter by letter? Or should teaching begin with the pattern of a familiar word which the child will learn to recognise by its shape and configuration?

The many experiments have proved that the differing abilities of teachers to apply different methods have led to inconclusive and confusing results. Vernon[1] says that experiments comparing different methods are not carried out for a sufficient period. The criticism is that claims are frequently made for one method or another because reading has improved to a greater extent on the average with one group but this has not occurred with another group using another method.

But when the children are tested after a follow-up investigation, there is frequently no significant difference in achievement between the two groups. Williams[2] has also emphasised the many problems involved in the experimental comparison of teaching methods.

Probably the proponents of the phonic method are correct in condemning the Look and Say method because it may involve too much mechanical drill. There is no doubt that a child must learn by considerable repetition in order to associate the shape of the word with the name attached to it. Probably the proponents of the Look and Say method are correct in condemning

[1] Vernon, M. D., 'The investigation of reading problems today', *Brit. J. Educ. Psychol.*, **30**, 2, 146–154, 1960.

[2] Williams, J. D., 'Some problems involved in the experimental comparison of teaching methods', *Educ. Res.*, **8**, 1, 26–41, 1965.

a pure phonic method which consists of boring drill in order to teach the blending of separate sounds. This can have very little interest for a child. Today, however, more and more proponents of the Look and Say method are recognising the value of phonics when phonic analysis is meaningful and applied to a whole word, preferably a word that a child has already learned to recognise at sight. More and more teachers are beginning to appreciate the importance of phonic clues, picture clues and context clues as tools to develop word recognition. I must emphasise that no one method is likely to provide the best results. What is more important is the teacher's own enthusiasm and faith in the methods being used. I have found that when children first learn to read there is no need for 'formal' phonics because if children are 'forced' into using word analysis at this stage, their attention to letters and their sounds will interfere with the ability to look for meaning in what is being read. Children at the beginning stage of reading learn to recognise words by their configurations.

I have obtained the best results by beginning with the Look and Say and Sentence Methods but introducing preparatory phonics at a very much earlier age than that suggested by many educationists including Bruce.[1] These preparatory phonics do not interfere with the child's ability to look for meaning in what he is reading because word analysis is not introduced at this stage.

I would dispute the contention of many investigators that children must have a certain mental age (usually six-and-a-half to seven-and-a-half years) before a real start on reading can begin. I would agree with a growing body of opinion that the tasks involved can be accomplished by many children at

[1] Bruce, D. J., 'The analysis of word sounds by young children', *Brit. J. Educ. Psychol.*, **34**, 2, 158–169, 1964.

surprisingly early ages.[1, 2, 3] I must mention, at this point, that my use of early phonics involves the occasional five minute period for phonic readiness activities and games as discussed in chapters 3 and 4. Many initial sounds may be taught in an incidental way. Eventually, as the children build up adequate working sight vocabularies, the periods devoted to more 'formal' phonics become longer (ten minutes) and more frequent (once a day). It is extremely important that phonic teaching is carefully graded, regular and systematic and it must not be regarded as reading when a child merely pronounces what the sounds say without realising the full meaning of what he reads.

I do not rely exclusively on seeing and hearing but include touch and movement. It is very important that children have the opportunity of finger tracing especially in the infant school so that they have the 'feel' of letters and words.

The ability to tackle unfamiliar words is a basic skill which must be acquired. A child will study the context and look for clues. He may recognise a word because of its pattern, length, initial letter, final letter or letter groupings. This leads to guessing and there is a danger that this habit may lead to indiscriminate guessing. In order to tackle unfamiliar words, a child must be able to associate the sound of a letter or letters with the printed symbol or symbols. A child must know the sound of individual letters, especially the initial letters of words. It is necessary for the child to have a knowledge of certain phonic combinations such as vowels and consonants – *an, en, in, at, it*; vowel digraphs – *oo, ee, oa, ay*; consonant digraphs – *ch, sh, th, wh*; consonant blends – *st, sp, bl, tr*. He must be able to analyse unfamiliar words and be able to recognise these phonic com-

[1] Downing, J. A., 'Is a "Mental Age of Six" essential for reading readiness?' *Educ. Res.*, **6**, 16–28, 1963.

[2] Lynn, R., 'Reading Readiness 11 – Reading readiness and the perceptual abilities of young children', *Educ. Res.*, **6**, 10–15, 1963.

[3] Doman, G., *Teach Your Baby to Read*, Jonathan Cape, London, 1963.

binations and, above all, be able to recombine these sounds in order to build up the word.

Unfortunately, many teachers are still suffering from the misconception that phonic teaching must consist of boring word-drill and too many are unaware that phonic teaching can include many interesting discovery activities and games which are fully enjoyed by children. I have found that those children who have been given the opportunity of participating in preparatory phonic activities and training benefit immensely in that they become more confident and better equipped to help themselves in reading at a later stage.

The phonic method of teaching reading has been criticised because the English language contains so many inconsistencies and many attempts have been made to overcome the fact that the correlation between sounds and symbols does not have a consistent one-to-one correlation. Many educationists, appreciating that English spelling is frequently inadequate and ambiguous, have looked for new approaches which give children more phonetic assistance. Diacritical marks[1] have been used to indicate that a vowel may either make the sound of its name, e.g. *gāte*, *wīne*, *rōse* or make a shorter sound, e.g. *căt*, *sĭt*, *pŏt*.

Colour has also been used as an aid to the recognition of the sound value of letters by several educationists including Moxon,[2] Gattegno,[3] Jones,[4] and E. & W. Bleasdale.[5] Sir James Pitman's i.t.a.[6] is yet another attempt to overcome the inconsistencies of the English language.

---

[1] Fry, E., 'The diacritical marking system and a preliminary comparison with ita', *The Second International Reading Symposium*, Cassell, 1967.

[2] Moxon, C. A. V., *A Remedial Reading Method*, Methuen, London, 1962.

[3] Gattegno, C., *Words in Colour*, Educational Explorers, London, 1962.

[4] Jones, J. K., *Colour Story Reading*, Nelson, London, 1967.

[5] Bleasdale, E. & W., *Reading by Rainbow*, Moor Platt Press, Bolton.

[6] The i.t.a. Foundation, 9 Southampton Place, London, W.C.1.

But, even considering these inconsistencies, it is interesting to study the remarks of Diack,[1] 'An alphabet is a system of symbols for sounds and these sounds are written down in the order in which the sounds are made. A printed word is a time-chart of sound. The act of reading is the act of translating these time-charts into the appropriate sounds, the sounds being associated with things, events or emotion.'

Phonic analysis involves the ability to identify the sounds of the English language, the symbols devised to represent them and the ability to associate sound with symbol. But to equip a child with a knowledge of phonics and to ignore other skills will limit his fluency and efficiency in reading. Reading is more than translating symbols into speech. Surely, the ability to read means that one is able to get ideas and information from the printed word.

Gulliford[2] states that the development of recognition skills requires a well-planned programme of phonics teaching and he suggests that one should keep three aims in mind: 'The first aim of teaching phonics is to ensure that the child recognises phonetic regularities in the spoken English words; the second, that he appreciates certain regularities in the written pattern or spelling of English words; the third aim is to associate these spelling patterns with particular sounds.'

[1] Diack, H., *In Spite of the Alphabet*, Chatto & Windus, London, 1965.
[2] Gulliford, R., *Backwardness and Educational Failure*, N.F.E.R., London, 1969.

2

A Suggested Order for Teaching Phonics

Roberts[1] has emphasised the earliest skills a child must learn when starting to learn to read. The child must recognise that 'the different letters vary in shape and that the shape of each letter is invariable. This can be achieved in a variety of ways – alphabet books, playing with wooden letters, matching individual letters, tracing with the forefinger letters made of glue and sand – much of it incidental and unstressed as part of learning to read.'

Sounds and phonic rules should be taught through the use of words and, whenever possible, words contained in a child's sight vocabulary and/or a child's own speech vocabulary. Even though I refer to the various letters in isolation, I do not wish to imply that letter shapes and sounds should be taught in isolation. It must be remembered that meaningful reading should be the aim on all occasions and exercises must be provided in order that children are able to apply newly acquired skills to new situations.

When phonic teaching is based on a child's sight vocabulary and language experience, it means that a child is taught to recognise whole words, for example, 'dog', before he is taught the sounds of symbols 'd', 'o' and 'g'. At the beginning stage of reading, the word dog is more meaningful than the three symbols of which it is formed. The foundations of phonics are established once the child has acquired a number of sight words and the

[1] Roberts, G. R., 'Criteria for an early reading programme', *Reading Skills: Theory and Practice*, U.K.R.A., Ward Lock Educational, 1970.

11

teacher brings the child's attention to the sounds associated with the initial letters of these known words.

It is important that sounds are learned within the whole word because it is impossible to tell the sound of a certain letter, except for its pronunciation in the word in which it occurs. It is impossible to know that the letter 'a' out of context stands for the sound as in 'c*a*t', '*a*te', 'w*a*ter', '*a*ll', 'c*a*re', '*a*re', 'w*a*s', '*a*bout'. It is impossible to know that 's' out of context stands for the sound of 'z' as in 'i*s*', 'sh' as in '*s*ure', 's' as in 'bu*s*' or have no sound at all as in 'i*s*land'.

Because I suggest a particular order for teaching phonics, I do not imply that this order is the only one that should be followed. I do not suggest that the steps involved in this suggested order are of equal importance in learning to read or that each step requires the same amount of teaching time. There is one major issue involved in deciding the order in which phonics should be taught. If one is to teach sounds and phonic rules in order of difficulty, should one include, at the beginning stage, those sounds which the children will encounter most frequently in their reading books and in their sight vocabulary? Unfortunately, the digraphs which children master quite easily and those sounds and phonic rules which they frequently encounter in practice do not always occur at the same time. I appreciate that even though I have found my suggested order for teaching phonics satisfactory, many teachers will wish to make modifications. However, my suggested order does ensure a systematic approach.

I would suggest that the most common pronunciations should be learned first (children will have encountered many of these in their early sight reading and written work), and, then, as a result of adopting a systematic approach, the teacher can emphasise the various deviations.

1. *Initial Single Consonants* (i)
   't, b, n, r, m, s, d, c' (hard as in 'cat'); 'p, g' (hard as in 'goat').

2. *Short Vowels*
   (i) Initial sounds
       'a' as in '*a*pple', 'i' as in '*i*nk', 'e' as in '*e*gg',
       'o' as in '*o*range', 'u' as in '*u*mbrella'.
   (ii) Middle sounds
       'a' as in 'b*a*t', 'i' as in 't*i*n', 'e' as in 'p*e*t',
       'o' as in 'h*o*t', 'u' as in 'j*u*g'.
   (iii) 'y' as in 'bab*y*', 'fl*y*'.

3. *Initial Single Consonants* (ii)
   'f, l, y, v, h, w, j, k, z'.

4. *Doubled Consonants*
   'bb, dd, ff, gg', etc. including 'ck'.
   Two identical consonants make the sound of one consonant.

5. *Initial Consonant Digraphs*
   'ch, sh, th' (as in '*th*ree'), 'wh, th' (as in '*th*at'), 'qu'.

6. *Initial Consonant Blends*
   'st, sp, sc, sk, sl, sm, sn, sw',
   'br, cr, dr, pr, tr, gr, fr',
   'bl, pl, cl, fl, gl'.

7. *Vowel Digraphs*
   'ai, ay'   'oi, oy',
   'oo' (two sounds as in w*oo*d and f*oo*d),
   'oa', 'ow' (as in c*ow* and sn*ow*), 'ou' (as in ab*ou*t and r*ou*gh),
   'au, aw, al',
   'ee, ea' (as in b*ea*n and h*ea*d),
   'ew, ue',
   'ei',
   'ie'.

8. *Other Sounds for 'c, g, s'*
   'c' followed by 'e', 'i' or 'y' has a soft 's' sound
   'g' followed by 'e', 'i' or 'y' has a soft 'j' sound
   's' makes the 'z' sound as in 'ha*s*'.

9. *The Final and Silent 'e'*
   (i) Functionless role as in 'kettl*e*', 'jungl*e*', 'nois*e*'.
   (ii) Modifying role as in 'cak*e*', 'cabl*e*', 'bit*e*', 'bon*e*', 'tub*e*'.
       Special pronunciation of 'are' as in 'fare', 'ire' as in 'fire',
       'ure' as in 'pure'.

10. *Modification of Vowels by 'r'*
    A vowel followed by 'r' often makes a new sound:
    'ar' as in 'c*ar*', 'or' as in 'f*or*', 'er' as in 'sist*er*',
    'ir' as in 'g*ir*l', 'ur' as in 'b*ur*n'.
    Modification by 'w' as in '*w*arm', '*w*orm'.

11. *Silent Letters*
    'b, g, m, gh, k, l, p, t, w'.

12. *Prefixes*
    Including 'ab, ad, be, com, de, dis, en, ex, pro, re, sub'.

13. *Syllables*
    Including 'ing, ed, er, ly, es, tion, y'.

14. *Suffixes*
    Including 'ion, tion, ation, er, y, al, ent, ful, ity, ly, ure, ous'.

The following is a list of some of the important steps in the development of independent word recognition:

1. Provide children with experiences that will lead to a rich and varied language development.
2. Can the child speak in complete sentences? Is he able to

produce sounds correctly? Is he able to involve himself in conversation?

3. In the early stages, help the child to develop a sight vocabulary.
4. Provide abundant practice in visual perception and discrimination so that he will develop the ability to distinguish significant differences in the visual forms of words.
5. Teach children to acquire sight words by their general configuration and visual clues.
6. Help the child to use the context for identifying and recognising words.
7. Ascertain the child's ability to listen and to discriminate between sounds.
8. Give children the opportunity to develop the skill involved in following verbal instructions.
9. Provide abundant practice in auditory perception and discrimination.
10. Help children to establish a left to right attack on new words.
11. Bring to their notice similar beginnings and endings of words.
12. Introduce children to alphabetical order and the use of the dictionary by means of a picture dictionary.
13. Provide children with interesting games and activities so that a level is reached with certain sight words where the response is almost automatic.
14. Allow visual analysis of a word to precede the sounding and blending of parts.
15. Teach skills when they can be used to attack new words and when it is appropriate to a child's development in reading.
16. Teach phonics gradually and in an interesting way by means of rhymes, games and other activities.
17. Help the child to identify familiar parts of words. This

should be done before blending them and pronouncing new words.

18. As children progress in reading, they should be assisted in the recognition of new words by systematic practice in structural analysis. This helps them to break down more complex words into roots, syllables, prefixes and suffixes.

19. There should be further use of the dictionary so that the child may use it as an aid to the pronunciation and meaning of new words.

20. Reading should be developmental and continuous throughout all stages of schooling and provision should be made to fit the reading programme to the needs and ability of each individual child so that independence in word recognition is attained.

3

First Things First

Language Development

'Reading is a type of linguistic performance. It is a type of linguistic response that depends first of all upon the language control achieved by each particular individual reader. Learning to read must begin with and build upon the habits of that precise language control. Of course one can postpone learning to read until a greater measure of language control has been achieved; but, whenever learning to read begins, it must start with and build upon whatever habits of language responses exist for the learner at that time.'[1]

If the teacher wants reading to be enjoyable and meaningful then an attempt should be made to teach those words found in a child's day to day vocabulary. Experiences should be provided leading to a rich and varied language development which includes many words and ideas that will be met in the printed form. Teachers must appreciate the relationship between language development and the child's ability in beginning reading. This point has been emphasised by many educationists including Thackray.[2]

[1] Fries, C. C., *Linguistics and Reading*, page 186, Holt, Rinehart & Winston, New York, 1966.
[2] Thackray, D. V., 'The relationship between reading readiness and reading progress', *Brit. J. Educ. Psychol.*, **35**, 252–254, 1965.

We all appreciate that infants coming from homes that are intellectually and culturally adequate are able to acquire language efficiency quite incidentally. We also appreciate that children coming from culturally deprived homes and the intellectually slow are not so fortunate.[1, 2, 3, 4]

There is a growth in materials for stimulating the language development of children. The Peabody Language Development Kit[5] consists of lessons and materials for four mental age groups from three-and-a-half to nine-and-a-half years. The materials include pictures, stories, puppets, tape recordings and music and are designed to stimulate language and intellectual development. The lessons contain practice for a whole range of mental and language functions.

Bereiter and Englemann[6] describe a method of teaching children with severe language retardation who come from homes that are economically and culturally deprived. Their approach is to provide a rigorous programme of mental improvement rather than the wider approach we are accustomed to in a normal infant school.

The 'Talkmore' Project (Arnold)[7] has been developed to meet the demand of many teachers. It has been devised so that all children continue to increase their vocabulary during the early school years. It is useful supplementary material for use with pre-reading and reading schemes. The 'Talkmore' Project is particularly useful for children from culturally deprived

---

[1] Morris, J. M., *Standards and Progress in Reading*, N.F.E.R., London, 1966.

[2] Kellmer-Pringle, M. L., et al., *11,000 Seven-year Olds*, Longman, London, 1966.

[3] Goodacre, E. J., *Teaching Beginners to Read: Report No. 2*, Teachers and their Pupils' Home Background, N.F.E.R., London, 1967.

[4] Lewis, M. M., *Language and the Child*, N.F.E.R., London, 1969.

[5] Dunn, L. & Smith, O., *The Peabody Language Development Kits*, American Guidance Services, Minneapolis, Minn., 1967.

[6] Bereiter, C. & Englemann, S., *Teaching Disadvantaged Children in the Pre-School*, Prentice-Hall, N.J., 1966.

[7] *The 'Talkmore' Project*, E. J. Arnold & Son Ltd., Butterly Street, Leeds, LS10 1AX.

18

homes, for retarded and educationally subnormal children and for immigrant children.

The following is a selection of activities which I have found useful:

1. *Using the Tape Recorder*

The tape recorder can be used to help the children to listen carefully to patterns of speech. Withdrawn children may often be helped by giving them opportunities to record in private what they may wish to say and then playing the recording back to the class.

The teacher can encourage the children to describe things and events. The Remedial Supply Company[1] provide an excellent tape – *Pictures in Sounds* – which can be used to encourage children to listen to sounds and then describe the events portrayed.

Children should be encouraged to talk about their likes and dislikes, journeys they have made and so on.

2. *Instructions*

The teacher asks children to carry out simple instructions. For example, a child is told to walk to the door of the classroom, turn left, pick up the waste paper basket and put it near the right-hand side of the teacher's desk. The remainder of the class watch and listen carefully to see if an error is made. Instructions should be varied and gradually increase in difficulty. The teacher should make the instructions as interesting and amusing as possible. This activity encourages accurate listening not only on the part of the child carrying out the instruction, but also by the other children in the class.

3. *Story Endings*

The teacher reads a short story to the children, leaving it unfinished. The children are asked to give their own versions

[1] The Remedial Supply Company, Dixon Street, Wolverhampton.

of the ending of the story. For example:

Peter lived near the sea. One day, he was walking along the beach. Suddenly he saw ......

4. *Classifications*

Divide the class up into teams. Ask questions similar to the following:

What word can we use for all the boys and girls in the classroom?

What word can we use for everything we eat?

What word can we use for all the things we wear?

What word can we use for cat, cow, dog, horse, elephant and monkey?

5. *Talking About Pictures*

Children are encouraged to talk about a large, coloured picture. They are encouraged to discuss the main theme of the picture and the various actions taking place. The Chameleon Street Cellograph Picture Making Outfit (Philip & Tacey)[1] is extremely useful for this kind of work. When the Picture Making Outfit is used, children can build up a story by placing certain pictures on the Street.

Children should be encouraged to describe the colours used in various pictures and should be asked questions relating to the weather, the season and so on. A few children may be able to make up short stories of one, two or three sentences.

6. *Play Acting*

Children are asked to give simple lines for various parts in the dramatisation of a familiar story. Various situations and happenings may be acted. For example, at the doctor's, at the supermarket, at the dentist's, a television programme, personal happenings.

[1] Philip & Tacey Ltd., 69–79 Fulham High Street, London, S.W.6.

7. *What Would You Do?*

The teacher gives the children a certain situation and asks them who they would send for if, for example, a water pipe burst, soot fell from the chimney, their house was on fire or there was a gas leak.

8. *Describing Words*

The teacher attempts to elicit from the children as many descriptive words as possible. A familiar object is shown to the class, for example, a balloon and the teacher asks the following questions:

> Who can tell me what this is?
> What colour is it?
> What shape is it?
> Is it heavy?

The children's answers will provide such words as balloon, yellow, round, light, thin.

Visual Discrimination

I have found that many children require exercises in visual and auditory discrimination. I regard these exercises as very important in preparing the child for reading and my own thoughts on this subject are shared by several educationists including Thackray[1] who found that when relating various measures of readiness at five years to eventual progress in reading, there was a considerable relationship with measures of visual and auditory discrimination.

A knowledge of a child's skills in visual discrimination will enable the teacher to devise games and activities which will help the child's progress in this field. Test 4 of *Standard Reading Tests*[2] is a useful test of visual discrimination and orientation.

---

[1] Thackray, D. V., 'The relationship between reading readiness and reading progress', *Brit. J. Educ. Psychol.*, **35**, 252–254, 1965.

[2] Daniels, J. C. & Diack, H., *The Standard Reading Tests*, Chatto & Windus, London, 1958.

There are useful exercises contained in the work of Tansley[1] and Presland.[2]

The following games and activities ought to be useful:

1. *Matching Shapes*

The teacher cuts out various shapes of various sizes such as squares, rectangles, circles and triangles. The children are told to group them according to shape.

2. *Jigsaws*

Use two identical pictures. Cut up one picture into pieces of various sizes. Tell the children to put the pieces together to correspond with the other picture. Such jigsaws may vary in difficulty from three simple pieces to more complex ones, e.g. commercially produced jigsaws.

3. *Kim's Game*

Place four or five familiar objects on a tray, desk or table, and give the children a few seconds to look at them. Tell the children to turn their heads away and cover the objects with a cloth. The children have to remember as many objects as possible. Teachers may devise many other variations. The time allowed and the number of objects may vary so that the game is made easier or more difficult.

One may include exercises to develop the skill of identifying:
  similar geometric figures;
  geometric figures with slight differences;
  common objects with slight differences;
  letters or small words.

The child is asked to underline or colour the figure, letter, word or part of a word which is identical to the one in the rectangle on the left-hand side. See the following six examples.

---

[1] Tansley, A. E., *Reading and Remedial Reading*, Routledge & Kegan Paul, London, 1967.

[2] Hughes, J. M. & Presland, J. L., Applied Psychology and Backward Readers. Supplement: *Journal and News Letter*, Association of Educational Psychologists, 1969.

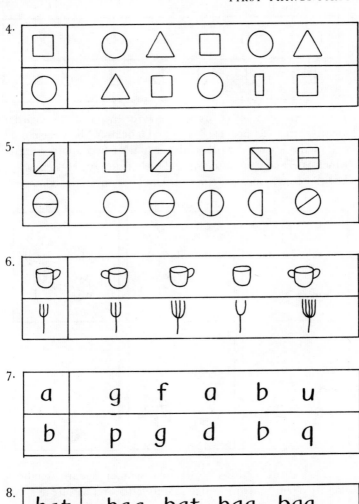

7.

a	g	f	a	b	u
b	p	g	d	b	q

8.

bat	bag	bat	bag	bag
dog	day	day	dog	day

9.

n	m	u	n	w	u
d	d	d	b	d	d

10. Prepare a set of six cards, as below, with two cards identical (see identical cards in 1 and 6 below). Show the child one of the identical cards and ask him to find another card which is exactly the same. Ask the child to give reasons why he has selected one particular card and not one of the others.

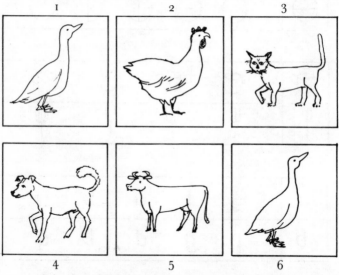

11. Ask the children to match symbol against symbol, picture against picture, letter against letter and picture against word, as in dominoes.

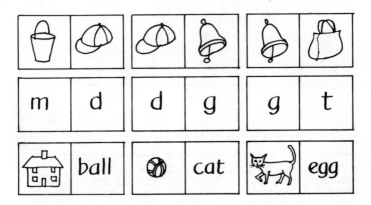

12. Provide the children with cards containing lines of similar symbols, objects, etc. Ask the children to underline the odd-man-out.

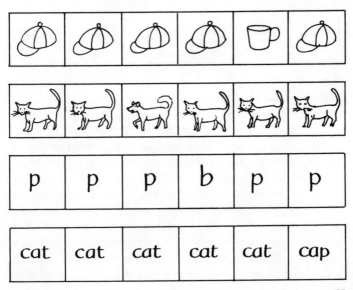

13. Provide the children with cards containing drawings of symbols, objects, letters, words with missing pieces. Ask the children to indicate what is missing from one square on each card. They may be asked to draw in the missing part.

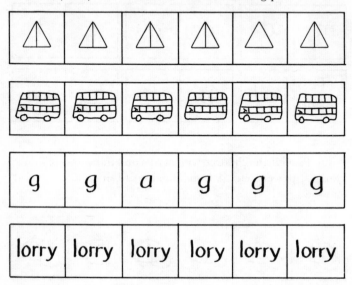

Auditory Discrimination

When a child begins to associate sounds with objects and does not confuse certain sounds that are similar such as 'Tommy', 'tummy', 'Tony' and 'tunnel' then he is beginning to master auditory discrimination. If a child is eventually to tackle phonic work then he will require this skill of auditory discrimination. If he is to attempt to 'unlock' a word which he has not met before, it will be necessary for him to appreciate that a word has its own sound pattern, that this pattern may be broken down into a series of sounds which are arranged in a definite sequence, and that these sounds relate to the shapes of letters or a combination of such shapes. Occasionally, a child may make progress in beginning reading as a result of relying on the look and say approach, but he will be unable to become a future fluent and independent reader if he does not have the ability to 'unlock' unknown words.

The following are a few suggestions for helping the child to develop the skill of auditory discrimination. Many others, involving rhymes and letter sounds, may be seen in chapter 4.

Useful tests for assessing auditory discrimination may be found in Test 6 of *The Standard Reading Tests*[1] and in the Wepman test.[2]

1. *High and Low Sounds*
High and low notes produced on a piano may help the child in specific discrimination. The teacher may produce a sound at different pitches. Teachers may think of many other ways of making different sounds.

2. *Everyday Sounds*
Ask the children to close their eyes and remain as quiet as possible. Then ask the children to listen for and remember as many sounds as they can, inside and outside the classroom. At first, the teacher may find that only a few children have heard many sounds, but, eventually, they will be able to report on – a passing car, a passing lorry, footsteps outside the school, footsteps in the school hall, laughter from a nearby classroom, whispering, sighing and so on.

The tape recorder may be used for a series of exercises. The Remedial Supply Company[3] supply tapes – *Pictures in Sound*, *Listening Tapes* and *Sound Discrimination Tapes*.

---

[1] Daniels, J. C., *The Standard Reading Tests*, Chatto & Windus, London, 1958.

[2] Wepman, J., *Auditory Discrimination Tests*, Language Research Associates, 1958.

[3] The Remedial Supply Company, Dixon Street, Wolverhampton.

27

3. *Guess Who's Speaking?*
The teacher selects a child to recite a well-known poem or nursery rhyme. The remainder of the class sit with eyes closed and attempt to discover the name of the child.

4. *Disguised Voices*
The teacher selects a child to recite a well-known poem or nursery rhyme. The child is told to disguise his voice as much as he can. The remainder of the class sit with eyes closed and attempt to discover the name of the child.

5. *Rhythms*
Percussion instruments may be used to help the children remember rhythms. The teacher may also tap out the rhythms and ask the children to repeat them. This may be followed by asking the children to march and dance to certain rhythms.

6. *Misfits*
The teacher calls out a series of words beginning with the same initial sound, but the series contains one word which has a different initial sound. The children are asked to put up their hands if they have detected the misfit. For example, 'bag, basket, bad, chair, bat'. Another variation is the use of rhyming words. For example, 'bit, hit, dog, pit, sit'.

7. *Recorded Sounds*
The teacher records many familiar sounds with the use of a tape recorder. For example, a knock on a door, clock chimes, the school bell, a door bell, animal noises. The children may either say what the sounds are or they may hold up a picture of the object.

8. *Two Pictures*
The teacher holds up two pictures at a time, e.g. an apple and a tap. The teacher says, 'Show me the tap.'

28

The children point at the picture of the tap.

Speed of response should be encouraged. Have two or more children and allow them to compete to see who is first. Put a slight emphasis on the initial sounds of the two words.

9. *Objects*
Show the children three objects, e.g. a basket, a pencil and a bat. Ask the children which two begin with the same sound.

10. *Objects on a Tray*
Place four or five objects on a tray and ask the children which one begins with a specific sound.

11. *Kim's Game*
The teacher places four or five familiar objects on a tray or desk. The children are allowed a few seconds to look at them. The children then turn their heads away and the teacher removes one of the objects. The children have to state the missing object and are encouraged to answer as follows, 'The missing object begins with the same sound as bat. It is bag.'

There are many variations of this game. The time allowed and the number of objects hidden or taken away may vary so that the game is made easier or more difficult. The game may eventually be extended to illustrate final sounds and vowel sounds in the middle of words.

12. *Listening Walks*
During nature walks or other out-of-door activities, children are asked to remember as many sounds as they can during periods of 'listening'. This may be discussed back in the classroom.

13. *Riddles*
You sleep in it and it begins with *bĕ*.
You ride in it and it begins with *că*.
You drink it and it begins with *mĭ*.

14. *Tongue and Lip Movements*

In some exceptional cases it may be helpful to show a child what tongue and lip movements are involved in making a particular sound.

15. *Hearing Tapes*

These tapes are supplied by the Remedial Supply Company. They were originally intended to be a form of training to improve discriminating ability but their greater use is for diagnostic purposes, to find out if this disability exists and, if so, at what point and at what degree.

Left/Right Orientation

It is very important that during the beginning stage of reading children learn that the eyes move from left to right across the page. The majority of children learn the correct sequence without difficulty through incidental learning, through activities involved in play and bodily activities and this may be the reason why teachers may neglect this very essential skill. Some children come to school needing specific practice in this skill before making an attempt at reading. They may have poor perceptual attack. They may begin at the right-hand side, miss out the initial letter, or may begin in the middle of the word and move either to left or right. This skill must never be taken for granted by the teacher because if it is not mastered then a child may exhibit many harmful reading habits including omissions, reversals, missing lines, etc. All activities involving hand-eye motor co-ordination will help. This may be done through games and playing with toys. Many other activities may be used such as tracing, folding along a line, joining dots, cutting out shapes and cutting along a line.

The teacher should provide the child with series of action pictures which have to be followed from left to right. Comics and Annuals contain such action pictures which are arranged from left to right. Other examples may be found in non-verbal intelligence tests. Eventually, the child may be given separate action pictures which he has to arrange in correct order from left to right in order to understand the sequence of the story. Certain individual pictures may help to encourage the left to right movement of the eye.

The Schonell and Standard Reading Tests include groups of words that may be used with children who have difficulty with the orientation of letter shapes and a left/right attack.

Here are a few further suggestions:

1. *Individual Pictures*

2. *Mazes*

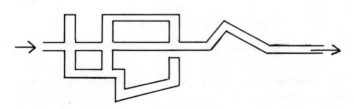

3. *Rearranging Pictures*

Provide the child with three or four pictures which tell a story if arranged correctly from left to right. Place the pictures in an incorrect order and ask the child to place them in such a way that they tell a story. Then ask the child to tell the story.

4. *Left/Right Cards*

Divide a piece of card, 24 cm × 6 cm, into six divisions, 4 cm wide, Illustrate the progression involved in making an object like a boat. Ask the children to tell you how the boat is made.

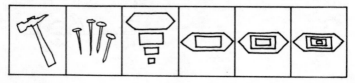

5. *Strip Stories*

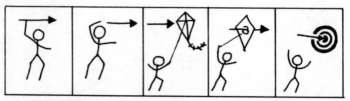

6. *Putting in Order*

Ask the child to put a few known words in the correct order and read out the sentence.

4

Early Phonics

'The teacher's task is to know how and what the child is learning and so to organise activities that success is achieved, at however modest a level. Thus the child is encouraged and stimulated to make further efforts. Goals must be individual if proper account is to be taken of individual differences.'[1]

There are certain abilities which children should have in order to understand and be able to apply phonic analysis and synthesis. They should be able to appreciate rhyme and rhythm, discriminate between letter sounds, blend sounds and associate a sound with its visual representation.

Because a child may be limited in the number of words he can commit to memory, some skill in phonic analysis and synthesis is essential. Eventually, the child must be able to analyse a word into its sounds and then be able to blend sounds to make whole words. At all stages of reading a child will encounter words that are unfamiliar, therefore, exercises and practice in the fundamentals of phonic work are essential.

[1] Learning to Read, *Reports on Education*, No. 64, 1970.

Rhyming

1. *Group Rhyming*

The teacher begins by saying aloud a certain word, e.g. 'cake'. The children have to think of words rhyming with this word. This continues until all the possibilities have been exhausted.

2. *Rhyming Cards*

Children match the pictures of objects and animals whose names rhyme.

3. *Rhyming Words*

When children appreciate what is meant by rhyme, as a result of using nursery rhymes, they may be asked to tell you the word which does not rhyme with three others.

The children are told to listen very carefully and the teacher reads from lists similar to the one below:

(i) bell, shell, gun, well;
(ii) ball, fall, fill, wall;
(iii) ring, bang, sing, wing;
(iv) coat, boat, mat, goat;
(v) bin, pin, man, win;
(vi) train, rain, chain, fun.

4. *A Rhyming Game*

Prepare a card, 10 cm × 8 cm, and divide it into two halves. On the left-hand side print four words from the child's sight vocabulary. Select four other words so that four pairs of rhyming words may be formed. Print these four words on pieces of cardboard, 3 cm long by 1 cm wide. Shuffle the cards and ask the child to pair them with words that rhyme.

fly	cry
bread	head
rain	train
sail	nail

5. See *The Use of the Tape Recorder* in chapter 6.

6. *Matching Cards and Charts*

Prepare a chart containing sixteen pictures of objects that may be divided into eight pairs of rhyming objects. The teacher calls out the word 'bell' and a child comes out and points at an object with a name that rhymes with bell. A further approach is to provide individual cards. The child has to place them in pairs according to rhyme.

7. *Classifications*

Provide a large envelope or bag containing pictures or objects. Ask the child to classify the objects according to whether they rhyme with each other. A further step is to ascertain whether the child is able to associate the various classifications with the printed symbols for their sounds. If pictures are used, the words may be printed on the reverse with the rhyming sounds underlined.

Initial Sounds

Phonic teaching should start in the pre-reading period and extend through all the stages of reading. It should be appreciated at this point that the phonic teaching during the pre-reading period will be very elementary and consist of the activities already discussed.

While a child is building up a sight vocabulary, he is also learning the sounds that initial letters give to words. If reading for meaning, based on a whole word approach, precedes phonic teaching, then the early phonics programme (or readiness for phonics), may run concurrently with the programme in beginning reading. Thus a beginning reader will not be impeded by the letters and their sounds while he is concentrating on the meaning of the sentence being read. All preparatory phonic work should be incidental to the overall reading programme.

At this stage, it should be remembered that because initial consonants are always blended with the adjacent vowel in a spoken word or syllable, these consonants are never heard apart from the adjacent vowel sound. One should keep this in mind when using the following suggestions with children. The first three activities give children an opportunity to hear like beginnings in words when both the initial consonant and the adjacent vowel sound alike. I suggest that the teacher should begin by providing as many activities as possible along the lines suggested. Then, when using the other suggestions, whenever

37

possible, children should not be asked to sound the letters in isolation. Many adaptations of the following suggestions may be used to help children learn initial sounds.

1. *Objects in the Classroom*

The teacher pronounces only the beginning of the name of the familiar object which can be seen in the classroom.

> I can see something and it begins with *dĕ*.
> The children answer – desk.
> I can see something and it begins with *tā*.
> The children answer – table.
> I can see something and it begins with *pĕ*.
> The children answer – pen.

2. *Animals*

> My cat would like to catch a *mou*.
> The children answer – mouse.
> I'm thinking of an animal that gives us wool and begins with *shē*.
> The children answer – sheep.
> I'm thinking of an animal that builds a nest and begins with *bir*.
> The children answer – bird.
> I'm thinking of an animal that quacks and begins with *dŭ*.
> The children answer – duck.

This approach may be adopted with many names of objects, plants and animals.

A further approach is to pronounce words and ask the children to give the beginning sounds.

> Tell me the sounds at the beginning of horse.
> The children answer – *hor*.
> Tell me the sounds at the beginning of girl.
> The children answer – *gir*.

3. *The Same Beginning Sounds*

The teacher pronounces a well-known word and asks the children to give the name of another beginning with the same sound. The teacher may use the word 'bun' and then ask the children to give the name of something that begins with *bŭ* and tells the children that we blow them.

The children answer – bubbles.

The teacher may continue as follows:

Think of something we ride in. (bus)
Think of something we put on bread. (butter)
Think of something that is small, has wings and flies. (butterfly)
Look for something we have on our clothes. (buttons)

Many words may be used in this way.

4. *'I Can' Game*

This is a game that can be used time and time again when certain letters of the alphabet are left out. The first child is asked what he can do with a word beginning with 'a', e.g. I can '*a*dd' with 'a'. The second child is asked what he can do with a word beginning with 'b', e.g. I can '*b*ite' with 'b'. When it is the first child's turn once again, new words must be used.

5. *Eat and Drink Game*

This is similar to the game above but on this occasion the children have to think of something to eat or drink beginning with 'a', then 'b' and so on.

6. *Christian Names*

Ask the children to say the names of boys and girls in the class whose names begin with a certain letter. Later, ask the children to write them.

7. *Names of Objects in the Classroom*

Ask the children to name objects beginning with certain letters.

8. Illustrate as many initial letter sounds as possible by preparing cards with drawings on the right-hand side and the initial letter on the left-hand side.

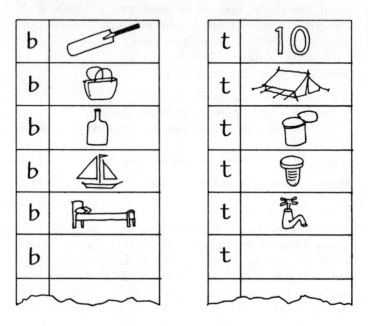

9. The teacher selects three words from the sight vocabulary of the children, e.g. 'bee', 'ball', 'big', and asks, 'Who can give me another word that begins with the 'b' sound?'

The teacher is supplied with further words, e.g. 'boat', 'bat', 'bag', 'bird'. The teacher adds these words to the list on the blackboard. He then asks, 'Can we see something that is the same in all these words?' The children answer that all begin with 'b'.

10. Ask the children, in turn, to say a word beginning with a certain letter. In the beginning, this may prove difficult but,

eventually, the children will attempt to prevent the activity from breaking down.

11. When several consonants have been learnt, children can sort flash cards into piles according to their initial letters.

12. Provide the children with pages of old books or magazines and let them ring the letter or letters being learned. Let the children cut out certain letters from newspapers. It must be remembered that children will require a great amount of practice in hearing sounds. The teacher must provide opportunities for the children to listen to many words beginning with particular sounds.

13. Ask the children to look at a picture containing actions or things and ask them to point at activities or objects beginning with a particular sound. This may also be carried out with a child's drawing.

14. Prepare cards containing the names of common objects seen in the classroom. Arrange these so that all cards containing the same initial letter are put together, e.g. 'ball, basket, bat, bag, bell, bottle'. Give each separate set to members of a group. Call out the words and ask the children to deliver them to the objects. Because each child is dealing with one initial letter, the teacher may, at the end of the activity, ask each child whether she noticed something 'special' about her own words.

15. The teacher writes several consonants on the blackboard, e.g. 'f, t, s, b'. She says a word and a child is asked to point at the letter on the blackboard which gives its 'beginning' letter.

16. Provide a row of five pictures and ask the child to place

counters on those pictures whose names begin with the same letter as the name of the object on the left-hand side.

17. Using words from the child's sight vocabulary, provide a picture of a well-known object with its name. Ask the child to mark all the words beginning with the same letter as the name for the picture.

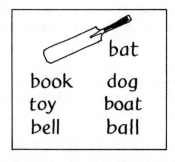

18. Prepare cards illustrating sight words and print each word under each picture. Provide the child with sufficient plastic or cardboard letters to make the words on the cards. Place the letters in a bag. Let us consider the word 'dog'. The child has to feel for the initial letter 'd' and place it on the initial letter on the card.

19. The teacher uses sight words and places flash cards at

the bottom of the blackboard or in a position where they may be seen by the class. She pronounces a word and asks a child to pick up a card containing a word which begins with the same sound as the one pronounced. The teacher calls out 'cat' and the child selects 'cap'.

20. The teacher and children cut out pictures of common objects from various newspapers and magazines. The teacher decides on the pictures to be cut out, depending on the emphasis she wishes to place on certain initial sounds. The pictures are sorted so that objects beginning with the initial sounds 't, b, c' are together. The words are already known as sight words. The teacher gives the pictures out to a group of children so that each child receives the same number of pictures, beginning with the three initial sounds. The teacher writes a word on the black-board, e.g. bag. The child with a picture of a bag brings it to the teacher. The object of the game is to get rid of all one's pictures.

21. In a list of six words, five begin with the same initial letter. The teacher reads them out and the children have to find the stranger. For example, 'kettle, kite, kangaroo, lorry, kipper'. The same activity may be used with rhyming words.

22. The teacher reads out sets of four words and asks the question, 'Which words begin with the same letter as in ten?'

   (i) dog, tap, bun, television;
  (ii) tent, fox, tip, monkey;
 (iii) tap, cow, table, horse;
 (iv) ball, tin, fire, top;
  (v) tub, pen, saw, Tom;
 (vi) boat, Tony, house, tea.

23. Provide a large envelope or bag containing pictures or small objects. Ask the child to classify objects according to their

initial sounds. A further step is to ascertain whether the child is able to associate the various classifications with the printed symbols for their initial sounds. If pictures are used, the words may be printed on the reverse of each card with the initial sounds underlined.

24. The teacher draws various pictures and then cyclostyles them. If possible three or four sheets of pictures should be available. The initial letters for all the pictures on one sheet are printed at the bottom. The child has to select the initial letter for each picture. He prints this under each picture. The teacher may vary this activity by printing the appropriate words under the pictures, but with the initial letters missing. The child has to find the missing letter and print it in the correct place in order to complete the word.

25. Cut out several pictures from magazines. Provide the child with pictures of three objects beginning with the same initial letter and three beginning with a different one. Provide the child with cards containing the initial letters or with plastic letters. The child has to place the correct letter on each picture.

26. Put a list of words without initial letters on the blackboard. Point at each word and read it and ask the children to suggest the missing letters. (Use sight words.)

(b)all	(p)ig	(m)ilk	(d)og
(c)at	(b)at	(r)ed	(y)ellow

27. Prepare cards containing two columns of three words each. Ask the child to draw a line from one word on the left to a word on the right which begins with the same sound.

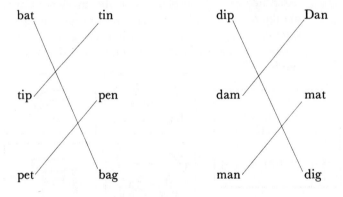

28. Ask children to tell you the word that begins with a different letter from three others. The children are told to listen carefully and the teacher reads from lists similar to the ones below:

   (i) bat, bell, cat, banana;
   (ii) fox, fire, fight, table;

45

(iii) jelly, house, jump, jam;
(iv) lorry, king, lamp, long;
 (v) man, match, mother, play;
(vi) tap, top, ten, dog.

29. *Riddles (using Sight Words)*

(i) Print a short riddle on the blackboard. Ask the children to draw the answer. (A further exercise would be to ask the children to copy the riddle and draw the answer.)

> I am round
> I grow on trees
> You eat me
> I begin with *a*

(ii) Ask the children to cut out pictures selected by you. Put three or four in an envelope. Write a simple riddle describing one of the pictures on the envelope. Carry out this procedure with several envelopes containing the same number of pictures. Children are given the envelopes and have to select the one picture that fits the riddle.

> I have four legs
> I have a tail
> I bark
> I begin with *d*

(iii) On a piece of card, 10 cm × 10 cm, paste a picture from a magazine or produce a simple line drawing. On the reverse of the card print a riddle about the picture. Number each line of the riddle. Then cut the card so that each line of the riddle is a separate strip of card.

The child places the strips containing the lines of the riddle in order and attempts to solve the riddle. The child may then turn over, keeping the strips in the same order, and check his answer.

1	I have two legs
2	I can sing
3	I can fly
4	I begin with **b**

1	I am round
2	I am very big
3	I am in the sky
4	I warm you
5	I begin with **s**

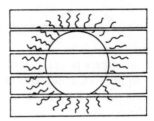

(iv) Ask the children to make their own riddle books. Encourage them to write riddles of three, four or more lines according to their ability. They should draw the answer to each riddle on the back of each page. The teacher should encourage them to write the word if this is possible. An alternative would be to allow the children to paste 'answer' pictures on the back of each page. When the riddle books are completed, the children may exchange them with members of the class. Children find this a very enjoyable exercise.

30. *Missing Words*

Using words from children's sight vocabulary, prepare illustrated sentence cards with certain words missing except for the initial letter. Children have to find the missing word from three or more. The correct word is placed over the initial letter on the sentence card.

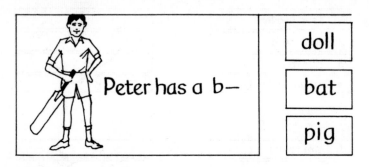

31. *Sound Lotto*

Cut out six pieces of card, 16 cm × 16 cm (or as many cards as required). Cut out 'key' pictures, 5 cm × 8 cm, from a magazine and paste a key picture at the top of each card. You then divide the remainder of the card into six blank spaces. Then cut out other pictures each showing an object with a name beginning with one of the initial sounds of the key pictures. Paste these pictures on pieces of card. Give one key picture to each child. The other smaller cards are shuffled and placed face down on the desk or table. A 'caller' picks up the first card and names the object portrayed. Each child must listen carefully, identifying the initial sound and whenever his key picture begins with the same initial sound, he claims the card. The winner is the first child to cover six blank spaces.

32. *Anagrams*

Sheets of cards are prepared containing drawings or pictures. Opposite each picture or drawing the appropriate word is printed, but the letters are scrambled. Children have to unscramble the letters and make the correct words.

33. *Individual Snap*

A pack of cards, each 10 cm × 6 cm, is made as follows:

One card has a drawing of a bird. The word 'bird' is printed at the top right-hand corner of the card with the initial letter 'b' cut out. Another card without a drawing has 'b' printed at the top left-hand corner. When the card with a drawing of a bird is placed on top of the other card, the word 'bird' is formed. (A self-correcting method may be adopted if one card is placed correctly on top of the other and a V shape is cut out. This V shape may be cut out at various other positions when other cards are being made.)

34. *Phonic Cards*

Prepare cards with a picture on one side together with its name (less the initial letter). On the reverse side print the initial letter.

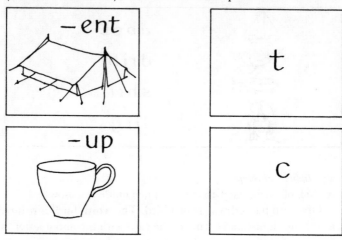

35. *Phonic Worksheets*

(i) Prepare cyclostyled sheets containing five drawings on each line and an initial letter at the beginning of each line. The child has to put a ring around the drawing or drawings with the name that begins with the initial letter on the left-hand side of the worksheet. (See worksheet 1, opposite.)

(ii) Prepare cyclostyled sheets containing drawings on the left-hand side and five different letters on the right-hand side opposite each drawing. The child has to find the initial letter of the name of the object and draw a ring around it. Do the first line for the child.

If the teacher finds that children are experiencing difficulty with certain initial sounds then the worksheets can be so planned that there is more emphasis placed on these sounds. (See worksheet 3, page 52.) Other worksheets may be so planned that they help in diagnosing specific difficulties.

Worksheet 1.

Worksheet 2.   *Worksheet 3.*

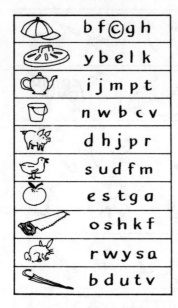

36. *Hearing Tapes*

These tapes are supplied by the Remedial Supply Company. It has been found that many children failing in reading have some difficulty in letter sound discrimination even though tests have found that a child may not be suffering from deafness. It is common for such children to have difficulty with initial sounds. These tapes have been devised to improve discriminating ability and for diagnostic purposes.

37. *A Pictorial Alphabet*

The use of a pictorial alphabet can assist children in their learning of initial sounds. The following pictorial alphabet was prepared by the students of Caerleon College of Education. Here an attempt has been made to produce a drawing of an object, animal, etc. in such a way that it represents the shape of the initial letter of its name. When the pictorial alphabet is used, the association of an initial letter with a picture (as used in Stott's *Programmed Reading Kit*[1]) is further assisted because the child may be able to remember the picture which is drawn in such a way that it represents the configuration of the initial letter. This pictorial alphabet contains the following:

apple, banana, cat, drum and drumstick, elephant, fish, girl, house, Indian, jet, key, log, mittens, nails, orange, pipe, queen, road, snake, tap, umbrellas, vase, worm, yacht and zip.

Various games and activities taken from my suggestions may be used if the pictorial alphabet can be cyclostyled on thin cardboard so that more than one copy of a letter is produced.

A Pictorial Alphabet

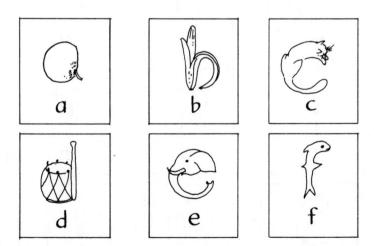

---

[1] *The Programmed Reading Kit*, Holmes-McDougal, Edinburgh.

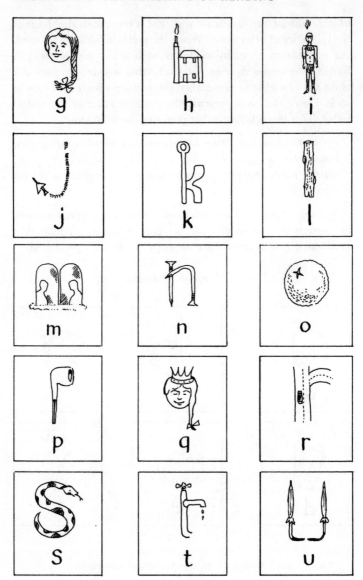

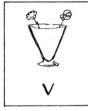

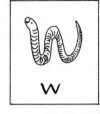

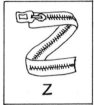

Final Sounds

Many of the games and activities suggested for the teaching of initial sounds may be used in modified form for the teaching of final sounds. Here are a few further suggestions:

1. Children may be helped to learn final sounds through the use of rhymes. The teacher says the word 'day' and asks the children to say words with the same sound. The teacher may write these words on the blackboard so that the children may appreciate the combination of letters which gives the same sound, e.g. 'day, Fay, gay, hay, lay, may, pay, ray, say and way'.

A further variation is to print sight words on small cards. Four teams are given an equal number of cards. The first player reads from his cards and if another player has a word that rhymes, then he must give the card to the first player. The winning player is the one with most cards at the end of the game.

2. The teacher writes several words on the blackboard, e.g. ring, sing, cold, wing, gold, sold. The teacher asks the children to come out and join those words ending with the same sound.

3. Cut out cards, 15 cm × 15 cm. On these cards paste pictures cut out from magazines. Under each picture print its name with the final letter missing. At the bottom of the card print all the missing letters. The child has to select the correct final letter for each word. Another approach is to prepare similar work and cyclostyle several copies of each card. In this case, the child may write in the missing letters.

4. *Riddles*
Use the various approaches as suggested for teaching initial sounds.

5. *Individual Snap*
See Initial Sounds.

6. *The Same Final Sounds*
The teacher pronounces two or three words and asks the

children to listen to the sound at the end of each word – 'tap, mop, cup'. He asks, 'Do these end with the same sound?'

Then the teacher pronounces two or three words with different final sounds – 'top, boat', and asks, 'Do these words end with the same sound?'

The teacher reads from a list of words and the children answer yes or no after each pair:

(i) boat fat;	(ii) bill hill;	(iii) mat man;
(iv) bed bad;	(v) tin pit;	(vi) dog dig.

7. Provide a large envelope or bag containing pictures or small objects. Ask the child to classify objects according to their final sounds.

A further step is to ascertain whether the child is able to associate the various classifications with the printed symbols for their final sounds. If pictures are used, the words may be printed on the reverse with the final sounds underlined.

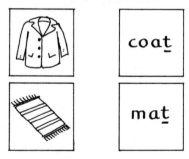

8. The teacher reads out sets of four words and asks the question, 'Which word ends with the same sound as mat?'

  (i) cat, chair, man, pot;
 (ii) pin, bat, torch, boat;
(iii) cot, shoe, foot, dress;
 (iv) net, toy, dog, pet;
  (v) table, nut, spot, bed;
 (vi) rat, lamp, wall, pit.

9. Using a selection of words taken from the child's sight vocabulary, arrange them in pairs so that both begin with the same initial letter but end with different sounds. Cyclostyle the lists of words. The teacher reads out the word that contains the final sound she wishes to emphasise and tells the child to underline this word:

(i) ball   bed;   (ii) hid   house;   (ii) rabbit   red;
(iv) God   go;   (v) ship   shed;   (vi) bread   brown.
(The teacher reads bed, hid, red, God, shed, bread.)

10. Using sight words, prepare illustrated sentence cards with certain words missing except for the final letters. Children have to find the missing word from three or more. The correct word is placed over the final letter on the sentence card.

11. *Phonic Cards*

Prepare cards with a picture on one side together with its name (less the final consonant). On the reverse side print the final letter of the word.

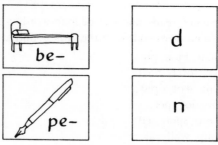

5

Moving on with Phonics

'There are many advantages to be gained when the emphasis in beginning reading is on pupil learning rather than on teacher instruction. Yet the creation of a school environment designed to promote motivated, individualised learning should not lead to the conclusion that all instruction should be taboo.'[1]

Vowel Sounds

Teachers very quickly appreciate that the teaching of vowel sounds may become quite a challenge because of their many inconsistencies. When rules are given, exceptions are many. Fortunately, many children reach correct conclusions before a rule is actually taught. Having read many words ending in 'e' through the whole word approach, these children conclude that the 'e' is not sounded and that the sound of the first vowel in the word is long, as in 'cake, make, gate, late, bite, kite, bone, throne, tune, tube'.

[1] Southgate, V., 'The importance of structure in beginning reading', *Reading Skills: Theory and Practice*, page 82, Ward Lock Educational, 1970.

Some teachers advocate that long vowels should be taught first, but it is more logical to teach the short sound because many words contained in a child's sight vocabulary will have the short vowel.

It is advisable to keep in mind the principle of moving from the known to the unknown. Use should be made of the words in a child's sight vocabulary. Some will contain short vowels and others long vowels. The teacher should draw the child's attention to the vowel sounds in these known words.

Short Vowel Sounds

The following procedure for learning the short sound for 'a' will serve as an example to show how children may discover all the vowel sounds. Each sound is introduced by using sight words in which it occurs. For example, the 'ă' sound in 'at, as, and, apple, cat, black, bag and hat'.

Let us consider the short 'a' as in 'cat'. This known word is printed on the blackboard or wallchart. The children are told to listen carefully to the word as they pronounce it. Ask the children what sounds they hear at the beginning of 'cat'. Those children who have had practice at sounding the beginning sounds of words as in the early exercises for initial sounds will answer că. Then ask the children what sound they hear at the end of că. The children answer ă. Children should be asked to select other words from their sight vocabularies which have the ă sound. Having learned the short 'a' sound, children can associate the sound with its letter as they work out new words. Now the children should be introduced to new three-letter words containing the short 'a' sound. At first, use these words orally for auditory exercises.

Long Vowel Sounds

Let us consider the long 'a' as in 'gate'. This known word is printed on the blackboard or wallchart. The children are told to listen carefully to the word as they pronounce it. Ask the children what sounds they hear at the beginning of 'gate'. Those children who have had practice at sounding the beginning sounds of words will answer *gā*. Then ask the children what sound they hear at the end of *gā*. The children answer *ā*. Children should be asked to select other words from their sight vocabularies which have the long 'a' sound. Having learned the long 'a' sound, children can associate the sound with its letter as they work out new words. Having read many words ending in 'e' through look and say, many children conclude that the 'e' is not sounded and that the sound of the first vowel in short words is long.

Rules for Vowel Sounds

1. A vowel followed by a consonant in a word or syllable usually has the short sound, e.g. 'pen' in 'pencil'.
2. Long vowels usually have their names as sounds.
3. A vowel which completes a word or syllable usually has a long sound, e.g. 'be, so, polo, total, pupil, bicycle'.
4. In short words containing two vowels and containing a final 'e', the final 'e' is usually silent and the preceding vowel is long, e.g. 'cake, bone, bite, tube'.
5. Vowels followed by 'r' usually have a blended sound, e.g. 'car, fur, fern, fir, corn'.
6. The vowel 'a' followed by 'l' or 'w' usually has a blended sound, e.g. 'ball, claw'.
7. If 'y' is at the end of a word containing no other vowel it has the long sound of 'i', e.g. 'by, sky, fly'.

Here are a few suggestions for helping the child to learn vowel sounds:

1. *Phonic Cards*
Prepare cards with a picture on one side together with its name (less the vowel). On the reverse side print the missing letter.

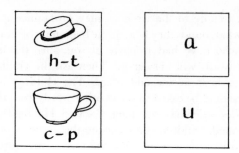

2. Strip Cards

Prepare strips of card containing five pictures. Print the names of the pictures under each one but leave out the vowel. Print the vowels at the bottom of the card. The children have to point to the missing vowel for each word. A further exercise is to ask the children to write out the words.

3. Find the Vowels

Prepare cards with a picture on one side together with its name (less the vowels). On the reverse side print the whole word and underline the vowels. Use sight words.

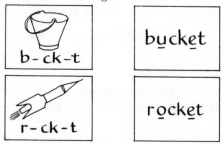

4. *Classifications*

Provide a large envelope or bag containing pictures or small objects. Ask the child to classify objects according to their middle vowel sounds. A further step is to ascertain whether the child is able to associate the various classifications with the printed symbol for their middle vowel sounds. If pictures are used, the words may be printed on the reverse side with the middle vowel sounds underlined.

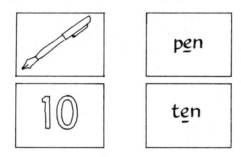

5. *Sentence Card*

Using words from a child's sight vocabulary, prepare illustrated sentence cards with certain words missing except for the middle vowel sound. Children have to find the missing word from three or more. The correct word is placed so that it covers the middle vowel on the sentence card.

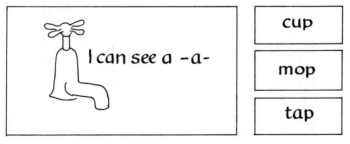

6. See *Programmed Reading* in chapter 6.

Substitutions and Blending

Substitutions

A very important skill is involved in substituting known letter sounds in unlocking unknown words. A child's sight vocabulary may contain such words as 'bang' and 'sang' and he should be able to use the 'r' sound, which he knows from such words as 'ran, rat, red, run, and rain', with *ang* in 'bang' to make 'rang'. Many important words may be read independently when a child knows certain sight words containing frequently used letter combinations if he is able to substitute sounds. Consider such words as 'game, cake, ring, hat, tin, and ball'. These words contain familiar sound combinations and many words may be recognised by substitution: '-ame, -ake, -ing, -at, -in, and -all'.

A child's sight vocabulary may contain such words as 'man, dog, pin, log, and beg'. He should be able to use the 't' sound, which he knows in words such as 'bat, cat, cot, hot, and boat', by substituting the sound at the end of these words and read 'mat, dot, pit, lot, and bet'.

1. *Substitution Cards*

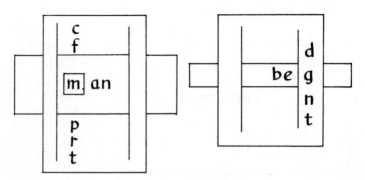

2. *The Substitution Wheel*

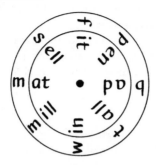

Blending

An essential part of learning to read is the ability to remember sounds in sequence and to blend into words. Once a child is able to identify three letter sequences, he has made a very important step towards acquiring essential skills in phonic reading. I would suggest that the teacher should adopt the approach of either 'to-p' or 't-op' for 'top' rather than 't-o-p'.

1. *Blending Cards*

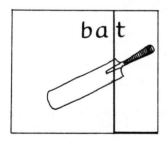

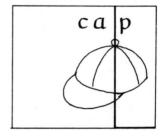

2. *Picture Cards*

Prepare several picture cards with the appropriate words printed under each one. Supply the children with the necessary plastic letters to complete these words. Let us consider a card with a picture of a jug.

65

Put the three letters in front of the child in the incorrect order, e.g. 'ugj'. Then select the initial letter. Ask the child to match the plastic letters with the printed ones on the card and then say the word. Let the child complete the other cards without your assistance. A further approach is to put the plastic letters in a bag so that the child has to feel for the appropriate letters.

3. *Simple Words*

Use simple words found in children's sight vocabulary, e.g. 'an, am, at, in, and'. Begin by making as many words as possible from these words ensuring that you can illustrate all the words. Print the words on the left-hand side of a sheet of paper and draw each picture on the right-hand side. Cyclostyle these if possible.

at	
bat	
cat	
hat	
mat	
rat	

The child may test himself by covering up the pictures and saying the word. The child checks his response by uncovering the picture.

Lists may be made from these words especially with those that cannot be illustrated:

an, ban, can, Dan, fan, man, nan, pan, ran;
am, ham, jam, mam, Pam, ram, Sam, tam;
in, bin, fin, pin, tin, win;
it, bit, hit, lit, pit, sit;
and, band, hand, land, sand.

From this beginning, one can lead on to other phonic combinations, e.g. 'ad, ag, ap, ar, ay, ed, eg, en, er, et, id, ig, im, ip, ir, og, op, or, ot, oy, ub, ug, un, ur, ut'.

4. *Riddles*

On a piece of card, 10 cm × 10 cm, print a word diagonally. On the reverse side of the card print a riddle about the word. Number each line of the riddle. Cut the card so that each line of the riddle and each letter of the word are on the same separate strip. The child places the strips containing the lines of the riddle in order and attempts to solve the riddle. The child may then turn over the strips of card, keeping them in the same order, and read the answer. A further approach is to allow the child to turn over each strip as he reads a line. The word will then be built up as the child proceeds.

p	
	u
	p

1	I have four legs
2	I have a tail
3	I am a baby dog

t	
	a
	p

1	I am in a house
2	You turn me
3	Water comes out

5. *Blending Cards*

hen	men
he[n]	me[n]

pen	ten
pe[n]	te[n]

67

The next three exercises from Stott's Programmed Reading Kit[1] are very useful and they should give teachers ideas for producing further apparatus keeping Stott's approach in mind.

6. *Half-Moon Cards*

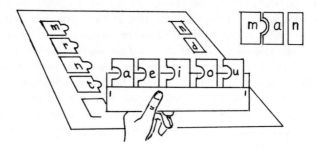

The basic purpose of the Half-Moon Cards is to help the child to use his knowledge of single-letter sounds and to convert them into phonic sight habits of two and three sounds. The child unlocks words by using their natural parts rather than breaking them up into single sounds. The traditional method of building up the word 'bat' by means of 'b-a-t' is avoided when the Half-Moon Cards are used. The known sounds 'b' and 'a' are placed together in the interlocking half-moon. The sounds are fused into *ba*. The teacher assists the child in the blending of *ba* with 't' by slightly emphasising the *ba* sound and sounding the 't' without too much emphasis. Stott suggests that the chief aim of the Half-Moon Cards is to teach the idea of taking two sounds in one act of perception. Reis[2] suggests a similar activity to Stott's Half-Moon Cards. A number of children are given letters of the alphabet which they hang around their necks. The teacher gives a signal and the children move the letters of a word together making the sounds of their respective letters until the whole word is formed.

[1] Stott, D. H., *The Programmed Reading Kit*, Holmes-McDougal, Edinburgh.
[2] Reis, R., *Fun with Phonics*, Cambridge Art Publishers, 1962.

7. *Two-Letter Cards*

The chief aims of the Two-Letter Cards are to teach the main two-letter word-parts as phonic sight habits and to bring the child's attention to the middle of the word so that he does not limit his attention to the beginning letters.

Two players are given five cards each. They are placed as in the illustration above in such a way that the child who is going to ask the other where a particular object is, is able to see all the pictures but the child opposite can only see the word parts. When the child is asked to point at the card which has 'parrot', he is confronted with 'p' on every card – 'pe, pu, po, pa, pi'. So the child has to pay attention to the second letter in order to select the correct one. A counter is awarded if the child selects the correct card.

8. *Port-Holes*

These give further practice in helping the child to establish the phonic sight habits of two-letter word-parts. It involves the same exercise as Two-Letter Cards but is a different activity.

Each child has a card containing 'port-holes'. One child holds up his card so that he can see his pictures but the other child can only see the word-parts on the reverse side of the card. The children ask each other where certain pictures are and the child answering pushes his pencil through a port-hole. If he is correct, he wins a counter. (The whole words are printed underneath the pictures.)

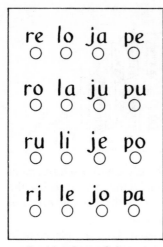

9. *Rotating Letter Cubes*

Cut out 1 cm wooden cubes from balsa wood or some other material. Drill holes through the centres of these cubes. Print letters on each side of each cube. The teacher should give some thought to the letters he wishes to print on the cubes to ensure the combinations he requires. The aim is to provide sets of three cubes so that words may be built up either letter by letter or by adding different initial letters or final letters to a sound contained in the first word made. Thread the sets of cubes on pieces of plastic curtain rail or pieces of elastic. The cubes may be turned around and many different words will be made.

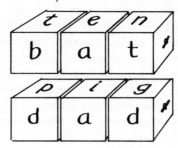

10. *Word Sums*

The teacher writes the first nine letters of the alphabet on the blackboard and gives each letter a number as follows:

a	b	c	d	e	f	g	h	i
1	2	3	4	5	6	7	8	9

Words are written on the blackboard using numbers. The children have to decode and read the words.

2	1	7		2	1	4		8	5	1	4
b	a	g		b	a	d		h	e	a	d

11. *Fill the Space*

Print two letters on the blackboard or on a card. Leave a space between the two letters, e.g. b—t. The children are asked to write as many words as they can that begin and end with these letters. For example, 'bat, bit, boat, beat, boot'. If a competition is involved, award one point for each letter added.

Consonant Blends and Digraphs

Consonant Blends: '*st, sp, sc, sk, sl, sw, sn, sm*
                    br, cr, dr, pr, tr, gr, fr
                    bl, pl, cl, fl, gl'.

Consonant Digraphs: '*ch, sh, th* (as in *th*ree), *wh, th* (as in *th*at), *qu*'.

Children will experience extreme difficulty if they do not perceive consonant blends or digraphs as single units. In the word pram, the child finds it difficult to appreciate the sound *pr* by sounding 'p' and 'r' separately. It is very important that children see the various letter groups as single-sound units. There should not be too much delay in teaching consonant blends and digraphs and other letter combinations because, after all, children will encounter, early in their reading experience, such words as bread and throw and it is impossible to build up these words from a knowledge of simple letter sounds.

When a child first encounters the consonant blend *tr* in his reading, the teacher should help the child by providing examples of other sight words containing the same consonant blend, e.g. '*tr*ee, *tr*ain, *tr*am, *tr*uck, *tr*ap, *tr*ay'. The child will then appreciate that the sound for *tr* remains the same irrespective of the other letters contained in the word.

A consonant digraph is a group of two letters expressing one sound – *sh*, *ch*, *wh*, *th*, *ck*. Once again, if a child is having difficulty with a particular digraph, provide examples of other sight words containing the same consonant digraph, e.g. '*sh*op, *sh*ip, *sh*eep, fi*sh*, di*sh*, wa*sh*; *ch*urch, *ch*erry, *ch*in, pat*ch*, mat*ch*, dit*ch*; *wh*eel, *wh*ale, *wh*ite; *th*ree, *th*in, *th*umb, *th*en, *th*ere, *th*ey, mou*th*, too*th*, pa*th*; du*ck*, ba*ck*, bla*ck*'.

Encourage the children to make small booklets for word collection containing various consonant blends and digraphs.

Here are a few further suggestions:

1. The teacher pronounces words with the same initial blends, e.g. '*sh*op, *sh*eep, *sh*ed, *sh*ip'. Ask the children to tell you the beginning sound for these words. Then ask them to give other words with the same initial blends. Eventually the teacher may move on to three-letter blends.

2. Use riddles to teach those consonant blends and digraphs causing difficulty. For example, *sn*, *cl*, *pl*, *st*, *ch*.

   (i) I live in the garden. I am very small. I carry my house on my back. I begin with the same sound as 'snap, snore and snug'. (Answer: *snail*.)

   (ii) You see me in the circus. You laugh at me. I begin with the same sound as 'cloud, clap and clean'. (Answer: *clown*.)

   (iii) I am round. You eat off me. I begin with the same sound as 'play, please and place'. (Answer: *plate*.)

   (iv) I am made of wood. You walk up me to go to bed. I begin with the same sound as 'stone, stamp and steps'. (Answer: *stairs*.)

(v) I have four legs. You sit on me. I begin with the same sound as 'church, cherry and chop'. (Answer: *chair*.)

3. *Rotating Letter Cubes*

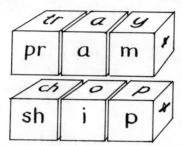

4. The teacher cuts out pieces of card, 8 cm × 5 cm. Three or more words are printed on each card. The child is able to see that identical sounds may be found in many different words.

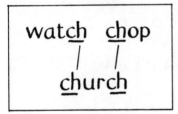 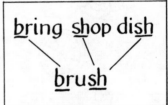

5. Ask the children to tell you the word beginning with a different sound from the other three. The children are told to listen carefully and the teacher reads from lists similar to the ones below.

(i) ship, shout, banana, shed;
(ii) wheel, whale, white, umbrella;
(iii) thin, thick, house, three;
(iv) there, table, that, then;
(v) chip, church, cow, chop;
(vi) stairs, dogs, steps, stones;
(vii) black, blue, blanket, ball;
(viii) pebble, grass, green, grape.

6. *Anagrams*

s o p o n

n i r a t

w a s n

g r o f

s l a g s

l a s n i

h e l e w

t w a c h

s e p e h

h e r e t

s h i f

c u d k

7. *Individual Snap*

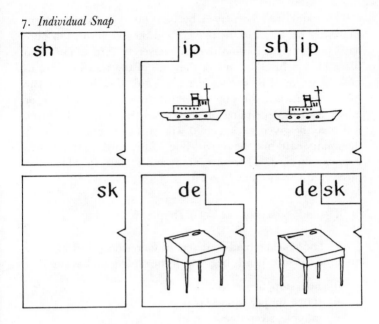

8. *Brick Wall Game*

Stott's *Programmed Reading Kit* contains a useful exercise for teaching consonant blends and digraphs. His Brick Wall Game has great appeal for children.

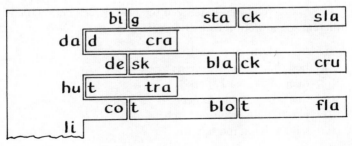

This game may be played by two, three or four children. Bricks are dealt out to the players and they keep them in piles with the letters uppermost. Each player in turn attempts to place his top brick on one of the ends of the wall in order to make a word. If he cannot make a word, then he places the brick underneath the pile and either uses the next brick or misses a turn, depending on the rules being used. The brick wall may be given to one child who wishes to build alone. A dictionary card may be provided at a later stage so that words may be checked. There are many other ways in which this piece of apparatus may be used.

9. See *Programmed Reading* in chapter 6.

10. The teacher reads out sets of four words and asks the question, 'Which words begin with the same sound as star?'

    (i) box, stop, fire, step;
   (ii) stairs, supper, stones, play;
  (iii) tadpole, steep, horse, stable;
  (iv) stumble, frog, stir, sweets;
   (v) chocolate, station, sheep, story;
  (vi) start, ambulance, stork, bus;
 (vii) sugar, storm, cheese, stem;
(viii) stay, boat, stocking, train.

11. Ask the children to tell you the word which ends with a different sound from the other three:

   (i) fish, splash, stop, wash;
  (ii) best, bangle, must, wrist;
 (iii) door, desk, mask, flask;
 (iv) duck, pencil, black, neck;
  (v) peach, book, church, larch;
 (vi) school, bath, moth, path.

12. *Blend Cards*

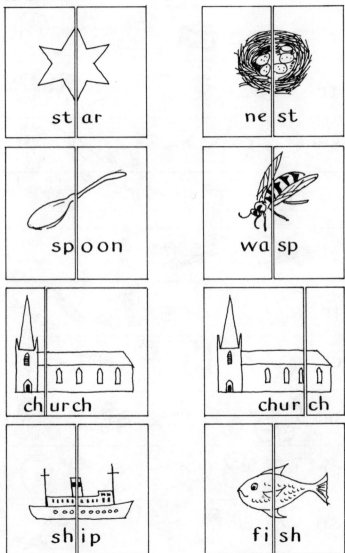

st ar

ne st

sp oo n

wa sp

ch urch

chur ch

sh ip

fi sh

13. *Worksheets*

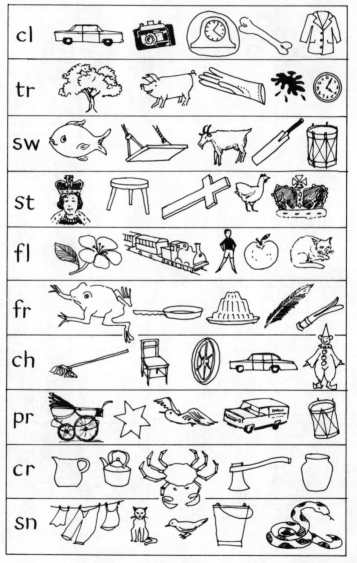

Prepare cyclostyled sheets containing five drawings on each line and a consonant blend or digraph at the beginning of each line. The child is asked to put a ring around the drawing or drawings with the name that begins with the sound on the left-hand side of the worksheet.

14. Prepare a piece of card, 8 cm × 2 cm, and divide it up into as many sections as required. Using words already known and containing initial consonant blends and digraphs, print one word on each section. For example, 'whale, sheep, church, bring, chips, glass, grass, chop, shed, train'. Cut out the words from the piece of card and then cut each word after each initial blend. Put these pieces in an envelope and ask the children to make the words.

15. Prepare four cards. On the left-hand side print the initial blend and on the right-hand side print a list of sound combinations. Children are asked to form words from each initial blend and sound combination.

16. Select words containing initial blends already known by the child. Place these words in a shoe-box. The child takes a card from the box and then has to think of another word beginning with the same initial blend.

17. *Matchbox Game*
Prepare small line drawings of objects with names that begin with various initial blends. These line drawings should be small enough to fit into a matchbox. Cover the one wide side of the matchbox with white paper. On this paper print the name of the object, less its initial consonant blend. Push out the left-hand side of the box and print the initial blend and then close the box. The child has to push out the box, form the word and attempt to read it. He can check his response by taking out the line drawing.

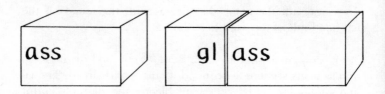

18. *Wooden Cube Game*

Take three wooden cubes. On one cube print the consonant blends *fl* and *tr* twice, and *sp* and *cl* once. On the second cube print 'a' three times and 'i' three times. On the third cube print 'p' and 't' twice and 'm' and 'n' once.

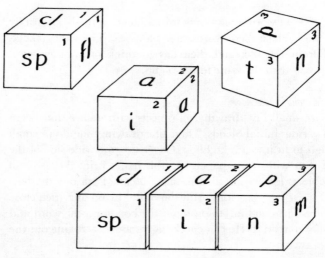

The children throw the cubes in the correct order, i.e. 1, 2 then 3, bring them together and attempt to make a word with the uppermost sides of the cubes. Provide a list of 'proper' words so that the children may check and see whether they have formed a correct word. The list for the above combinations would be 'flap, flat, flan, trap, tram, spat, span, clap, clan, flip, flit, trip, trim, spit, spin, clip'.

Various games may be used with these cubes and many other blends may be taught using this approach.

A selection of words containing consonant blends and digraphs that may be illustrated is given below:

bl	blue, black, blot, blanket, blossom, block, blind, blizzard;
cl	claw, clock, cloth, cloud, clown, class, clay, climb, cling;
fl	fly, flower, flag, flames, flour, flock, floor, flakes;
gl	glass, glove, glue, globe, glitter, gleam;
pl	plate, play, plant, plum, platform, plank;
sl	sling, slug, slippers, sledge, slide, slip, sleeve, sleep;
br	bread, brick, brush, broom, bridge, brown, broken, branch;
cr	crust, crack, crowd, crab, crocus, crane, cross, crumb, cradle;
dr	dress, driver, drum, draw, drink, drain, drawer;
fr	fruit, frog, frame, frying, frozen;
gr	green, grass, grapes, gran, gravy, grocer;
pr	pram, prince, present, primrose, prunes, prize;
tr	tree, train, truck, traffic, triangle, trumpet, trousers;
ch	chair, church, chicken, cherries, chestnuts, chest, chin, chip, chop, china, chimney, chain, chisel;
sh	ship, sheep, shell, shed, shoes, shop, shoulder;
th	three, thorn, thimble, thumb, thick, thin;
th	father, mother, brother, leather, feather;
wh	wheel, whale, white, whistle, whiskers, whisk;
qu	queen, quiver, quilt, quarry, square;

sk	skirt, sky, skewer, skates, skip, skittles, skin;
sm	smoke, small, smell, smith, smash, smile;
sn	snake, snow-man, snail, snout;
sp	spots, spoon, spade, spout, spark, space-man;
st	star, stick, stamp, steps, stairs, stage, stable, sty, stag;
sw	sweets, swan, swing, switch, sweep, swift, swim, swallow.

Phonic Combinations

Adopt the general principles involved in the teaching of letter sounds. It is extremely useful to have books from various reading schemes in which almost all the words can be built up using the various phonic techniques known at this stage. The *Royal Road Readers*[1] contain a systematic approach together with Sullivan's *Programmed Reading*.[2] One may find that the exercises contained in these schemes are not sufficient and supplementary work will have to be provided. *Sounding and Blending*[3] is a useful supplementary book. The *Sound Sense* reading scheme,[4] *Sounds and Words*[5] and *Moving on with Reading*[6] are examples of reading books which emphasise phonic building and include sight words as well.

The following cards will be useful for word building with various phonic combinations. Certain combinations may create difficulty because they are frequently confused with each other, e.g. *ar, er, ir, or, ur*.

[1] *The Royal Road Readers*, Chatto & Windus, London.
[2] *Programmed Reading*, Sullivan Associates – obtainable from McGraw-Hill, London.
[3] *Sounding and Blending*, Gibson & Sons, Glasgow.
[4] *Sound Sense*, E. J. Arnold, Leeds.
[5] *Sounds and Words*, University of London Press.
[6] *Moving on with Reading*, Nelson.

1. *Phonic Combination Cards*

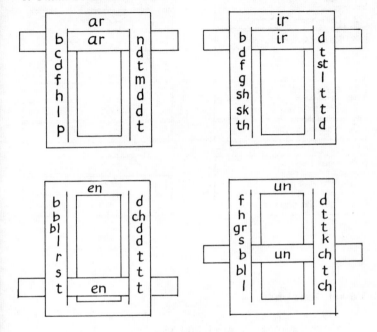

2. *Riddles*

Cut a piece of card into strips of equal length. Print the clues on the strips and on the reverse side print the letters of the word. Print the sound combination on the one strip. The child has to read the clues in the correct order and then turn the strips over and read the answer on the other side.

1 I am on the head of a cow	h
2 There are two of us	or
3 I have a sharp point	n

1	I am a small home		h
2	I am made of wood		ut
3	Rabbits live in me		ch

1	I am small		st
2	You lick me		am
3	You post me		p

1	I am food		l
2	You eat me		un
3	I am the second meal		ch

Vowel Digraphs

ai   ay   oi   oy

oo (Two sounds as in 'w*oo*d' and 'f*oo*d')

oa   ow (as in t*ow*)   *ou*

ow (as in c*ow*)   *ou* (also has *ow* sound as in '*ou*t')

au   aw   al

ee   ea (Two sounds as in 'b*ea*n' and 'h*ea*d')

ei

ie (Two sounds as in 'p*ie*' and 'ch*ie*f'.)

ew   ue

A vowel digraph is created when two vowels come together and represent a single sound. Usually when two vowels come together the first is usually long and the second silent. There are many exceptions but this is usually the case with *ai, ee, oa, ea, ay* as in 'n*ai*l, sh*ee*p, g*oa*t, m*ea*t, pl*ay*'. If the vowel *a* is followed by 'l' or 'w', then a blended sound results as in 'call, ball, awful, paw, claw'. When two vowels come together and are both sounded in the same syllable, they are called diphthongs as the *ou* in 'm*ou*se', *oi* in 'c*oi*n' and *oy* in 'b*oy*'.

There is the problem of more than one sound for some letters or letter combinations and the teacher must teach the child that certain letters will have these different sounds. I would suggest that the teacher should teach one sound for a letter or letter combination at a time and then eventually teach the alternative sound or sounds when the first sound is well known in the context of many words. If, for example, the two sounds for *ea* are involved, allow the child to encounter the first sound in sentences, e.g. 'I told Tom to sit on the s*ea*t and *ea*t the m*ea*t.'

Here are further suggestions for teaching vowel digraphs:

1. *Underlining*
Four sets of words are cyclostyled and a sheet given to each child. The teacher tells the children to underline the word she calls out. Use sight words.

  (i) mice, meat, match;
 (ii) steal, stop, step;
(iii) baby, bean, bed;
(iv) leaf, leg, little.

The teacher reads meat, steal, bean, leaf.

2. *Magazine Pictures*
Select pictures in magazines containing the vowel digraphs you wish to emphasise. Tell the children to cut out these pictures and paste them in their scrap-books. Ensure that you inform the children of the pictures you want pasted on certain pages. Ask the children to put up their hands if, for example, they have pictures with names of objects containing the *ou* sound. Ask the children to call out these words and write them on the blackboard, underlining the *ou* sound. Ask the children concerned to print *ou* at the top of the page and then copy the words from the blackboard and put them on the right-hand

side of each picture. Then proceed to the next vowel digraph.

3. *Picture Booklets*

The teacher should draw the child's attention to those vowel digraphs found in his sight vocabulary. Let him make booklets for each digraph with a key word and picture on the cover of each booklet.

The floating boat
The oa family

The noisy boy
The oi, oy family

4. *Vowel Digraph Cards*

Use a piece of card, 16 cm × 12 cm, and prepare a vowel digraph card as illustrated below. Print words which cannot be illustrated at the bottom of the card.

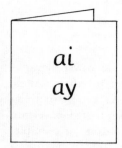

ai
ay

	train		hay
	tray		chain
	nail		pray
away	again	today	day

5. *Fill the Space*

Write on the blackboard the first and last letters of a word containing a vowel digraph. Use pecked lines for the missing letters, e.g. c--n (coin). Each child receives several cards with words containing vowel digraphs. The child with the word 'coin' reads the word and comes out to the blackboard to complete the word.

6. *Riddles*

1 I am wet in a tin	*p*
2 I have many colours	*ai*
3 You use a brush with me	*n*
4 I become dry	*t*

1 I have four legs	*m*
2 I have a tail	*ou*
3 I am very small	*s*
4 Cats run after me	*e*

7. *Individual Snap Cards*

8. See *Programmed Reading* in chapter 6.

Word Families

1. *Make the Word*

Prepare cards containing word families as follows:

> *ail, ain, oat, ead.*

Provide smaller separate cards containing initial letters. Initially, these smaller cards may contain an illustration, but eventually it may be left out.

	n	ail		ch	ain
t	ail		tr	ain
s	ail		r	ain
b	oat		h	ead
c	oat		thr	ead
g	oat		br	ead

2. *Word Family Cards*

f
l
n ight
st

f
h
m ail
p
r
st

3. *Rotating Letter Cubes*

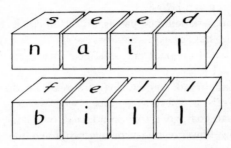

4. See *Programmed Reading* in chapter 6.

5. Prepare a card containing the word families being studied at the time, such as *ain, ake, ell, oat*. Print these word families three or four times on the card but ensure that they are in a mixed order. Provide an envelope containing initial single consonants or consonant blends and digraphs such as 'tr, b, r, c, b, sh, g, fl'. The child attempts to make as many words as possible by placing the initial letters in front of the word families.

6. Print ten words on the blackboard and ask the children to write them down in groups according to word families. The list may be as follows:

cake   tail
coat   goat
bell   bake
sail   same
game   shell

The groups will be as follows:

cake   coat   bell   sail   game
bake   goat   shell   tail   same

A selection of words containing vowel digraphs that may be illustrated is given below:

ai   snail, sail, pail, tail, paints, rails, train, nail, chain, rain;

ay   tray, hay, crayon, play, pray;

ea   tea, leaf, cream, bead, seal, meat, beach, teacher, bean, peach;

ea   head, bread, feather, thread, spread, heather;

ee   sweets, bee, feet, sheep, sleep, seed, weed;

oa   boat, coat, goat, toad, road, coal, oak, float, coach;

ow   cow, flower, clown, crown, gown, town, towel, shower;

ow   snow, bow, row, yellow, mower;

ou   house, mouse, cloud, scout, mouth;

al   ball, wall, fall, small;

au   saucer, sauce, saucepan, haul;

aw   saw, straw, paw, lawn, yawn, claw, shawl, drawer;

ew   screw, yew-tree, stew;

ue   flue, glue, cruet;

oi   oil, boil, point, coin, coil, soil, join;

oy   boy, toy, joy;

oo   spoon, moon, balloon, stool, school, tools;

oo   book, wood, cook, hook, foot, brook, soot.

Silent Letters

Children learn many words containing silent letters while building up a sight vocabulary. However, teachers should find it very useful to be aware of the various rules.

1. 'b' is silent when it comes before 't' and after 'm' as shown in the following examples:

       dou*b*t   lam*b*   thum*b*

       de*b*t   com*b*   clim*b*

2. 'g' is silent when it is followed by 'n' and 'm' as shown in the following examples:

       si*g*n   *g*nat   *g*nu

       rei*g*n   *g*naw   *g*nash

3. 'h' is silent when preceded by 'r', is frequently silent before a vowel and is never pronounced when it follows a vowel in a word or syllable, as shown in the following examples:

rhyme	hour	exhaust	ah
rhubarb	honest	exhibit	hurrah

4. *gh* is silent after the long vowel sounds of *i*, *ai* and *ei* and the vowel sound *ou* and *au* as shown in the following examples:

high	straight	eight	bought
night	weight	weigh	caught

5. 'k' is silent before the sound 'n' as shown in the following examples:

knife	knot	knock	kneel
knit	know	knew	knob

6. 'l' is silent when it comes before the sounds 'k', 'd' and 'm' as shown in the following examples:

walk	folk	palm	could
chalk	yolk	calm	should

7. 'p' is silent before the sounds 's' and 'n' as shown in the following examples:

psalm   pneumonia

8. 't' is silent when preceded by 's' 'f' as shown in the following examples:

listen	rustle	often
whistle	nestle	soften

9. 'w' is silent when it is followed by 'r' as shown in the following examples:

wren	wrist	wring	wrong
write	wrap	wreck	wrote

Allow the children to build up various families containing silent letters. For example:

bri*gh*t	fri*gh*t	mi*gh*t	si*gh*t
fi*gh*t	li*gh*t	pli*gh*t	sli*gh*t
fli*gh*t	ni*gh*t	ri*gh*t	ti*gh*t

Syllabication

Children should, eventually, be able to break down polysyllabic words into syllables if they are to pronounce words correctly, or as correctly as possible. A syllable is a vowel or a cluster of letters containing a vowel, and this makes one speech sound.

Teachers may find the rules for syllabication useful in helping to divide words into syllables but it must be mentioned that these rules have their exceptions. Children should not be taught the following rules. They should be provided with a number of examples and, if possible, allowed to form their own rules and express them in their own words.

The teacher may ask the question, 'What usually happens when one consonant comes between two vowels?'

Then the teacher writes a list of sight words on the blackboard similar to those below.

ti ger	o ver	ro bin
he ro	ro bot	fath er
mon ey	rock et	sta tion
be gin	co ver	pu pil

The rule will then emerge. If there is one consonant between two vowels, the consonant usually goes with the next syllable if the preceding vowel is long, and with the preceding syllable if the vowel is short.

The teacher adopts the same approach if he wishes to teach what happens when two or more consonants come between the vowels. The teacher writes a list of words on the blackboard.

win dow	rab bit	sum mer
ta ble	se cret	din ner
cot ton	pen cil	let ter
win ter	gar den	mas ter

The rule is that if there are two or more consonants between the vowels in a word all the consonants go with the next vowel if the preceding vowel is long; if the vowel is short, the first consonant stays with the preceding syllable and the others go with the following syllable. When there are two identical consonants between the vowel sounds the break comes between the consonants.

The following list of words shows how the division comes between two adjacent vowels.

gi ant	qui et	li on
ru in	fu el	du el

Many words found in a child's reading vocabulary are compound words and these are fairly easy to break up into syllables.

black board	tooth brush	grass snake
play ground	post box	rail way

The rule is that if a word consists of two complete words, the word is divided between the words.

It is important that children are able to recognise familiar units or parts of words such as prefixes, suffixes and root words. These are usually pronounced as units. Make a list of prefixes such as 'ab, ad, bi, com, de, dis, en, ex, pro, re, sub, in, un'.

*de*fend	*dis*miss	*ex*plain
*re*turn	*mis*take	*in*crease
*ex*port	*pro*gramme	*en*joy

List suffixes such as 'ed, er, est, ing, ful, ness, less, ish, tion'.

land*ed*	seat*ed*	act*ed*
teach*er*	farm*er*	paint*er*

old*est*	long*est*	soft*est*
runn*ing*	laugh*ing*	sleep*ing*
sad*ness*	glad*ness*	swift*ness*
use*less*	speech*less*	thank*less*
self*ish*	fool*ish*	child*ish*
sta*tion*	atten*tion*	frac*tion*

There are certain letter combinations found at the ends of words that are rarely divided but remain as the final syllable. The final 'e' is silent.

ap*ple*	un*cle*	can*dle*
an*kle*	sim*ple*	bot*tle*
mar*ble*	sin*gle*	puz*zle*

The Long Word Jigsaws contained in Stott's *Programmed Reading Kit* are very useful for this work.

6

Other Aids and Materials with a Phonic Bias

Programmed Reading

Programmed learning is an attempt to make learning as easy as possible. The material is broken down into a series of short steps. Programmed reading material demands constant activity on the part of the child because of a constant interchange between it and the child. The child is informed immediately of the success or failure of his response. He is able to use the material at his own pace and there is not the same time-lag as he would experience in the normal classroom situation where he has to wait for the teacher to attend to him.

The teacher must consider whether the content of the material holds the child's interest and whether the child is notified of his mistake and is able to correct himself. The teacher must also consider whether the written work involved is suitable for the child and reinforces his learning.

The following is a selection of programmed reading work cards. These have been selected from a graded series in order to show examples of the form of progression involved. The first example is devoted to the use of sight words and the teaching of initial sounds. Others involve purely phonic work. The answers are covered with a piece of card and the child may check his response by moving the card to the next line. The correct answer to the above line is found in the left-hand column.

Children may be told to either underline, ring or write the word where required.

1. *Sight Words and Initial Sounds*

	1 Here is the		b - - -
ball	2 Here is a		d - -
dog	3 I see the		h - -
hat			

2. *Initial Sounds*

	1 Here is a		hat / bat / cat
bat	2 Here is a		pan / fan / man
man	3 Here is a		hen / pen / ten
pen	4 Here is a		bin / pin / tin
tin			

3. *Final Sounds*

	1 I see the		map / man / mat
mat	2 We see the		cup / cub / cut
cup	3 Here is a		pet / pen / peg
peg	4 I see the		pin / big / pip
pig			

4. *Middle Vowel Sounds*

	1 Here is a		pin / pan / pen
pen	2 I see the		pit / pot / pet
pot	3 This is a		cut / cat / cot
cot	4 We see a		fin / fan / fen
fan			

5. *Consonant Blends and Digraphs*

	1 The pig has a big - - - - - ·	spout / shout / snout
snout	2 The boy gave the girl a - - - - - ·	sheet / sweet / sleet
sweet	3 I do not like - - - - - - ·	stakes / shakes / snakes
snakes	4 We use a rope to - - - - ·	slip / ship / skip
skip		

6. *Vowel Digraphs*

	1 We eat with a sp - - n	ou / oa / oo
spoon	2 We wear shoes on our f - - t	ea / ee / ei
feet	3 We put a cup on a s - -cer	ai / ay / au
saucer	4 We sailed up the river in a b - -t	ou / oa / ow
boat		

97

7. *Stories Involving Word Families*

	1 One day we went for a < walk / talk	
walk	2 We saw two boys having a < light / fight	
fight	3 One boy jumped on the other's < back / sack	
back	4 and both fell to the < pound / ground	
ground		

The Tape Recorder as a Phonic Aid

I regard the tape recorder as one of the most important aids to the teaching of reading. I have experimented with the use of the tape recorder as a reading aid for several years.[1, 2, 3, 4] If the teacher gives some thought to the ways in which she helps the individual child to read during a one-to-one teaching situation, then she can channel this approach to the provision of supported taped reading lessons. A reading situation can be created on tape so that the child will learn to read by reading.

If a tape recorder is available with an extension speaker socket, then individual headphones or earplugs can be plugged in and the children can be isolated from the various other activities of the classroom. The Remedial Supply Company[5] supplies earphones, tape players and an abundance of taped

[1] Hughes, J. M., 'Look, hear and say', *Forward Trends*, **10**, 1, 29–32, 1966.

[2] Hughes, J. M., 'Taped lessons to aid teaching of reading', *Teacher in Wales*, **8**, 16, 1–2, 1968. **8**, 17, 15–16, 1968.

[3] Hughes, J. M., 'Learning to read with the tape recorder', *Times Educ. Supp.*, 23 May, 1969.

[4] Hughes, J. M., 'The tape recorder as a reading aid', *Teachers World*, 15 August, 1969.

[5] The Remedial Supply Company, Dixon Street, Wolverhampton.

reading material. The Primary Audio Set[1] consists of a metal junction box which is plugged into the extension speaker socket. This box, which serves as a volume booster, has six connections to which six stethoscope-type headphones can easily be connected.

An incidental phonic approach may be adopted even when the recorded material is prepared mainly for a look and say approach. Occasionally, the teacher can bring the child's attention to the beginnings and endings of words. If written responses are required, it is wise to limit these to one-word answers or the ringing and underlining of words. The exercises previously discussed in the section on programmed reading can easily be adapted for use with the tape recorder. The following is an exercise involving rhyme:

The children are asked to listen very carefully to the five words in each line, then to listen to the three words on the right-hand side of their cyclostyled sheet and underline the one that rhymes with the other five.

	tell
1. bell, fell, sell, shell, well	tall
	till
	well
2. bill, fill, hill, mill, pill	wall
	will
	hell
3. ball, call, fall, tall, wall	hall
	hill

[1] The Primary Audio Set, Code No. 20 c 204, S. G. Brown Ltd., King George's Avenue, Watford, Hertfordshire.

	stung
4. ring, sing, bring, fling, swing	sting
	steps
	sheep
5. bead, feed, need, lead, weed	sell
	seed
	rod
6. bed, fed, head, lead, wed	red
	rid
	many
7. batch, catch, hatch, scratch, patch	match
	money

The teacher should ensure that the child is involved throughout the lesson by asking him to look, listen, read and answer questions. When books from a reading scheme have been recorded, it is useful to number the lines on each page so that the child can easily find the word to which the teacher wishes to draw his attention.

The tape recorder can also be used for more specific phonic teaching. Various phonic materials can be provided to assist the child in recognising individual letters, the relationship between letters and sounds and, eventually, blending sounds into words. The following books are very useful for use with the tape recorder and contain either a purely phonic approach or a phonic bias: *The Ladybird Key Words Reading Scheme* (Wills & Hepworth) beginning with 4c; *Sounds and Words* (U.L.P.); *Sound Sense* (E. J. Arnold); *Royal Road Readers* (Chatto & Windus); *Sounding and Blending* (Gibson); *Learn Your Sounds* (Blackie); *Word Families* (Philograph Publications) and *Programmed Reading* (Sullivan Associates – obtainable from McGraw-Hill).

The Clifton Audio-Visual Reading Programme[1] has a phonic approach and consists of forty reading cards which are used in conjunction with taped material. A supplementary writing programme has been developed to run parallel to the reading programme. There is also diagnostic material to assist in the determining of a pupil's initial level in the programme.

The Remedial Supply Company supply two very good tapes (*Phonics 1 & 2*). *Phonics 1* works in conjunction with simple apparatus and involves the teaching of single sounds, simple phonic blends and early digraphs. It is designed particularly for remedial work and takes into account the fact that most children who fail in reading know the letters by name but not by sound. The object is to teach the sounds basing the teaching on what is already known.

Phonics 2 covers simple and complex blending and syllabication. There are about 250 words and each one is matched with an illustration.

The English Colour Code Programmed Reading Course[2] is intended for remedial teaching. The words contained in this taped reading course are based on recent vocabulary studies. A computer study has been made of the frequency of the spelling patterns of the English language. This study has influenced the introduction of phonic rules.

This reading course does assume some ability in the recognition of individual letter symbols and the most frequent sounds of individual letters. Colour is used to assist the child in the learning of vowel sounds. There are fifty worksheets included in the reading course and these can be cleaned with a damp cloth.

The Programmed Reading Kit[3]

Parts of this reading kit have already been discussed in chapter

[1] *The Clifton Audio-Visual Reading Programme*, E.S.A. Ltd., Pinnacles, Harlow, Essex.

[2] Mosely, D., *The English Colour Code Programmed Reading Course*, N.S.M.H.C.

[3] Stott, D. H., *The Programmed Reading Kit*, Holmes-McDougall, Edinburgh.

5. The kit is a set of materials designed to impart phonic knowledge and to encourage the growth of phonic skills. The material is arranged into individual and group games which are largely self-corrective. The complete kit of thirty pieces is sufficient for a group of four or six children, or more if they are at different stages or progress at different rates. The material is used for playing games and is self-corrective so that a child teaches himself or a group will teach each other.

The learning processes involved in this kit are finely programmed so that the child may move on quite easily from one stage to the next. The kit has a very important attribute in that a class, at very different stages, may be kept occupied without needing constant attention.

The key to the method involved in the kit is the building up of phonic-sight habits.[1] The letter-sound associations are mastered naturally, and are acquired in an almost unconscious manner.

The kit is very useful because it may be used as supplementary material for any other approach or with any particular reading scheme. The most useful part of the kit is contained in the first fourteen items. The games contained in these items provide the amount of repetition needed for a thorough learning of essential phonic skills.

The Word Study Kit[2]

The Word Study Kit is used on conjunction with the Bell & Howell Language Master. It introduces children, who have acquired a sight vocabulary and the understanding of simple word-building with consonant and short vowels, to the association of sounds with certain groups of letters and to the building of more complex words.

The Word Study Kit includes 104 Language Master Cards divided up into five sets of cards, each card covering four words

[1] Stott, D. H., *Manual for the Programmed Reading Kit*, Homes-McDougall, Edinburgh, 1962.
[2] *The Word Study Kit and The Language Master 701*, Bell & Howell A-V Ltd., Alperton House, Bridgewater Road, Wembley, Middlesex.

containing a letter group known to be a particular area of reading difficulty.

Set 1	Blue	Initial Consonant Blends	sp	sk	dr	fr	pl
			squ	st	gr	thr	bl
			sc	pr	cr	sl	gl
			sw	br	tr	fl	cl

Set 2	Red	Short Vowels	a	u	u-e	oi	ea
		Long Vowels	e	a-e	oo	oa	ai
		Vowel Digraphs	i	i-e	oo	ee	ie
			o	o-e	ou	ea	ie

Set 3	Brown	Common Phonemes	an	ake	oy	ell	ight	ow
			and	all	et	ew	ing	ow
			at	aw	en	in	ot	un
			ack	ay	ent	ill	old	nk

Set 4	Green	Consonant Digraphs	th	ar	ur	-b	-ge
		Magic 'r'	sh	er	kn	c	y
		silent letters	ch	ir	wr	g	y
		soft 'c' and 'g'	wh	or	qu	-ce	ck
		Two sounds of 'y'					

Set 5	Black	Initial and Final Syllables	be-	pre-	com-	-le	-ous
			de-	pro-	dis-	-al	-tion
			re-	im-	-ful	-ure	-sion
			per-	ex-	-fully	-ment	-cious

The cards have a two-track magnetic strip of tape. One is for the teacher to pre-record the correct pronunciation; the other is for the child to record and compare his own attempts. The cards are simply 'fed' into the Language Master. The child is able to look at a whole word or phonic part within a word and hear the correct pronunciation. He can later record his own attempts and compare this with the teacher's track. *Burroughs' Vocabulary List* is used and the words chosen are those familiar to young children.

The Word Study Kit also contains Word Study Survey Sheets enabling the teacher to identify areas of weakness; four picture masks so that illustrations may be masked, showing the words only; four sets of playing cards, a set of bingo cards and a set of word dominoes; one copy of *My Word Study Book* and one copy of *Teacher's Notes*.

The SRA Reading Laboratory 1: Word Games[1]

The excellent SRA Reading Laboratories are so designed that children have a planned routine. They are designed to meet the needs of children of varying ages of ability in a given age group and to improve their reading skills of comprehension, vocabulary and speed.

Reading Laboratory 1: Word Games is designed for use with *Reading Laboratories 1a*, *1b* and *1c*, but is also extremely useful with any other reading scheme with a phonic basis. A phonic survey may be used by the teacher in order to show a child's strengths and weaknesses in phonics. The child may then be directed to those games which will provide him with the necessary exercises to overcome his weaknesses.

The 44 games contained in *Reading Laboratory 1: Word Games* cover 136 phonic and structural analysis skills and are played by pairs of children. Each child plays the word game listed in his programme and moves through these games at his own rate of learning.

Word Games provides an intensive and specific word-attack programme. It helps the child to develop mastery of phonic and structural word-analysis skills.

The Talking Page

The Talking Page[2] weighs about 7·25 kg and is about the size

[1] The SRA Reading Laboratories, Science Research Associates, Reading Road, Henley on Thames, Oxon.

[2] The Talking Page, Rank-REC Ltd., 11 Belgrave Road, London, S.W.1.

of a tape recorder. Specially designed books[1,2] are placed on the top and a disc is dropped into the slot at the rear of the machine and locked into position by pressing a button. Each page of the book is marked in such a way that the child may select passages by moving a lever. When this is done, the book and disc become co-ordinated and the appropriate audio message is heard. A stethoscope-type headphone may be plugged in and this automatically cuts out the internal loud-speaker.

The First Stage Reading Book is aimed at second year infant and first and second year junior children. The book is designed to represent a combination of look and say, phonic and alpha-betic teaching methods. The aim is to help children to acquire a reading vocabulary of approximately five hundred words, either singly or in sentence form, containing no phonic irregu-larities. He should also be able to read a selection of special words containing phonetic irregularities and eventually possess the necessary skills to decode many other words not yet en-countered. The approach is to postpone the necessity of dealing with the irregularities of English spelling until insight into the significance of letters has been achieved.

Patterns of Sound[3]
This system, involved in four books, is based on the relationship between recognition of the sounds of written alphabetical symbols and an understanding of how these sounds are pro-duced by lips, teeth and tongue. Kinaesthetic techniques are basic to the instruction through listening, looking and many movement activities. Each alphabetical symbol is introduced to the child in the form of an explanation of what the mouth has to do in making the sound.

[1] Diack, H., '*Jeff and Liz*'. *First Stage Reading*, Rank-REC Ltd., London, 1969.
[2] Gardner, K., '*Jeff and Liz*'. *Second Stage Reading*, Rank-REC Ltd., London, 1969.
[3] Baldwin, G., *Patterns of Sound*, The Chartwell Press, London, 1969.

The purpose of each page of the pupil's book is to ensure that he understands what the lips, tongue, teeth and breath are doing to produce the sound of a symbol. It is suggested that the problem of 'reversals' is less likely to occur when this approach is adopted.

Colour is used in these books to help the child read the symbols correctly. Games and activities are used to help the child appreciate a new rule or idea. Clapping, colouring in letters, ringing them with dots and other physical responses are used to help the child reinforce his memory.

7

Classroom Organisation

Beginning Reading

All activities and experiences provided for the child should be such that they encourage the child to want to read.

During the stage of reading preparation, the child should have experiences which will help to develop his powers of visual and auditory discrimination, his levels of spoken vocabulary, listening, and social and emotional maturity.

In the same way as children learn to speak as a result of living in an environment where speech is part of everyday life, so when they begin school they should enter an environment where the written word is part of everyday living. Children should be in a classroom environment where they are able to express their own ideas verbally and in drawing, painting, modelling, building and acting. The classroom should provide colourful books of all kinds, covering a wide range of interests. Children should be encouraged to handle books, look at pictures and talk about what they see. Here is the beginning of the convention of opening books at the beginning, turning the pages over in the correct manner and following lines of print from left to right.

The teacher reads stories, talks about pictures and encourages children to talk about them. Children should be surrounded by colourful and interesting displays and various objects carrying labels, phrases and sentences.

It is at this stage that the teacher provides opportunities for relating experiences and happenings with the written word. Various charts and notices will inform children of their various tasks, etc.

1. Mary — Weather chart and calendar
2. John — Sharpen the pencils
3. June and Jane — Milk
4. Brian — Feed the hamster
5. Jean — Flowers
6. George and Ken — Wash the paint-brushes
7. Ann — Drawing paper
8. Elizabeth — Clay

It is very important to remember that notices should be removed when they have served their purpose. If they are left on the walls too long, then children will ignore them because many become lost in the many pictures, charts, lists and so on.

The making of books is a very important activity in learning to read. Such books are made up from the child's own ideas, words and sentences. The teacher encourages the child to talk and write about as many interests and activities as possible so that the child builds up a vocabulary of words which are meaningful and interesting.

It is during this period that the teacher will be carefully observing her children and noting if they are:

1. developing favourable work attitudes;
2. showing persistence;
3. exhibiting powers of sustained attention;
4. able to recognise similarities and differences;
5. aware of spatial relationships when using jigsaws, toys, puzzles, lotto and dominoes;
6. showing an interest in books and a desire to read;

7. listening with attention to a story being read;
8. able to carry out verbal instructions;
9. exhibiting normal vision, hearing and motor control;
10. physically normal and do not tire easily.

Before or during the time children begin to read their first readers, it is suggested that they become accustomed to the words and characters in such readers. Many first readers have much supplementary material which will help to provide the necessary extra experience and practice. Many games and activities can be based on this supplementary material and other teacher-made material.

The teacher should study the various games and activities available, analyse the skills which they promote and the level of difficulty which they represent. A game or activity indulged in for too long a period without substitution of new items, can lead to overlearning of something known very well already. If the game or activity is such that a child can add new items and thus use forms of adaptation the value of the material is further extended.

The following are points which the teacher should have in mind when deciding upon the various reading games and activities which she wishes to use:

1. Do they provide exercises for the development of preparation for reading?
2. Do they place the onus of active learning on the child?
3. Do they help to establish word recognition?
4. Do they help in diagnosing a child's difficulties?
5. Do they involve activities concerning listening, speaking and writing?
6. Is learning carefully graded?
7. Are the various skills being taught rather than being tested?
8. Are the instructions simple and clear enough for the child to involve himself in the activity?

There are many arguments over the suggestion that reading may be taught before primary school age. Many teachers emphasise that children are not ready for specific instruction until a certain level of maturity has been reached. Others suggest that many children can and do read quite early. It is important that one should be aware of what is being done with children before they begin normal schooling. Doman[1] claims that he is able to teach babies to read.

It has been claimed that all children in Montessori schools learn to read and write before the normal school age. It is interesting to note a few of the approaches used in these schools.

The teachers start the *I-Spy* game as early as possible. 'This is the letter "B". Can you see anything beginning with the letter "B"? I spy a box. "B" is for box.' Gradually the children appreciate the sound of the letter. The children are given sandpaper letters which they use to trace over with their fingers so that they learn the shapes. This will help when they begin writing. The next step is to learn certain digraphs such as *ai*, *oy*, *sh*, *ch*, *wh*, and so on. They are given cut-out letters to play with and to make words.

Certain teachers suggest that parents could assist their children along the 'reading road' by teaching the alphabet using large wooden or plastic letters and making up games with them. When the alphabet is mastered, it is suggested that children should be taught to read simple words rather than short sentences. These simple words should be concrete nouns: names of objects which the child can see, hold, touch or feel. Labels can be pasted on these objects.

Organising the Reading

Class Reading
This is an approach which has generally fallen into disuse. A set of books is given out so that each child has the same book.

[1] Doman, G., *Teach Your Baby to Read*, Jonathan Cape, 1963.

The children read in turn and many stutter and stammer through their words because few children are likely to be at the same level of reading attainment.

Group Reading
Here the class is divided into groups of three to six with children having the same reading age. One child is usually appointed leader and the reading is frequently from the same text. Unknown words are either 'worked out' by the group or the leader asks the teacher. The teacher moves from group to group and spends most of her time with those children who are experiencing difficulties.

A leader of a group may be a child whose reading attainment is well above that of the remainder of the group. Several different texts may be used in the same group.

Group reading has its advantages in that children 'move on' without the direct supervision of the teacher. All members of the group are involved either reading or listening. Members of the group work as a unit because they share their knowledge.

There are, however, several disadvantages in group reading. There can be disciplinary problems and a teacher can spend most of her time keeping the groups under control and in their correct places. There is a danger that if the group leader is a far better reader than the rest of the group he may be held back. The varying interests and attainments of a small group may be quite substantial, so may the reading speeds. One child may struggle through his book whereas another loses patience because he wishes to move on more rapidly. This applies particularly when the same text is being used. A further point is that it is sometimes forgotten that reading aloud is frequently slower than silent reading.

It is more advisable to use groups for other reading activities such as reading games and reading apparatus.

Setting

In this approach a whole year group or maybe two or more year groups combine for reading activities. The most able groups could be quite large and could concentrate on silent reading. The remainder of the children could be graded into progressively smaller groups. The smallest group consisting of those at the beginning stage of reading or experiencing serious difficulties. The smaller groups could concentrate on specific reading skills. Promotion could be arranged so that the children would move up to other groups.

Individual Reading

The most valuable contribution to the teaching of reading is made when the teacher is in a position to give individual attention to the child. Teaching machines, tape recorders and other aids and media may cater to some extent for certain individuals, but they cannot replace the one to one approach of the teacher and the encouragement she is able to give.

It is at the beginning stage of reading that this personal contact is very important. Eventually, when the child's reading ability increases, personal contact will become less, but the child should not be neglected at the beginning stage and the teacher must make every effort to hear children reading as often as possible. This is the finest teaching situation when the crux of the child's reading problem may be fully appreciated.

Ideally, the teacher should listen to children reading every day, but it is fully understood that this is impossible with a class of between thirty and forty children. Even when a teacher attempts to listen to as many children as she can, she is naturally concerned about what the other children are doing. Games and activities, self-corrective materials, workbooks, teaching machines and other aids and media may be used to supplement the teacher's individual contact. This would also give the teacher the opportunity to attend to the poor reader who requires more personal attention.

If the teacher can find sufficient time just to listen to her children then she will be in a better position to fully appreciate any difficulties being experienced and attempt to assist the child by providing activities designed to overcome these difficulties.

It is advisable that one member of staff should specialise in the teaching of reading and take responsibility for organising and advising. It may be possible to have an 'adoption' system whereby each teacher adopts a poor reader whom she sees for ten minutes each day. In certain areas, Sixth Formers are encouraged to spend some time in primary schools as part of a particular study. Some have assisted poor readers. (This may be a rather delicate issue in certain areas.)

It is important that records are kept of a child's progress in reading. Frequently, the only record is a slip of cardboard recording the page reached by the child. This is not sufficient. A child's difficulties must be noted. Frequently, a teacher notices that a particular child is experiencing a certain difficulty. An attempt may be made at the time to assist the child, but then the difficulty may be forgotten because on the next occasion when the teacher listens to the child the child does not encounter the same difficulty in the text he is reading to the teacher, but the difficulty still remains.

Reading Schemes

It is now quite usual to provide a wide variety of reading books for children rather than have large numbers from one particular reading scheme. This approach provides children with broader and more general reading experiences. Books from various schemes are selected with different characteristics in order to meet the needs of individual children. All too frequently a child's reading ability is judged on the progress which he has made in a particular scheme and when he is given reading books or reading materials of comparable difficulty his reading attainment falls dramatically. It has become apparent to me that if a child is confined to the narrowness of one reading scheme without the opportunity of other varied reading experiences, then this is harmful to the child's growth and independence in reading.

A reading scheme may be put to its greatest use with children of average or below average ability. These are the children who require more time to master the various reading skills. It is useful because as the child moves through the scheme he provides evidence of his success and shows the teacher his progress and ability. A graded series provides a control over grading of vocabulary and content and helps the teacher to organise the reading in a class with a wide range of individual attainments.

A good reading scheme provides a means of controlled vocabulary and reading skills and so provides the child with a sense of security. It provides a basic sight vocabulary in the early stages with the vocabulary being based on the word frequency in the spoken language of the child.

A reading scheme should be looked upon as complementary to the teaching of the various reading skills. One cannot expect a child to learn these skills through one or two or more reading books if these books are to be interesting to the child.

Before a child is started on a particular reading scheme, use the supplementary material supplied with the scheme and, where appropriate, add to it so that he will become accustomed to the characters he will meet in his first book. Various stories may be told using these characters and involving the children in forms of dramatisation. Various games and activities may be used so that certain words become well-known before the child actually starts reading his first book. It should be remembered that the child should show that he is ready for his first reading book in the way in which he shows interest in reading, and that he wants to read. It is at this stage that the child is helped to develop his own vocabulary based on interests and activities through the making of individual and group books.

What makes a good reading scheme?

Do the books contain a genuine story element? There are a few well-established reading schemes with no genuine story content. These contain pages of illustrations with accompanying pages of words or phrases relating to the illustrations. The illustrations act as stimuli but the books cannot be regarded as reading books in the recognised sense.

Are the incidents and language in the early stages within the experience of the children? Does the content cater for present day interests and contain words used frequently in the natural conversation of children and in their written work?

Is the word list fairly short for the early stages? The first books should contain a limited but not limiting vocabulary. There should be an adequate number of new words to a page. These new words should be controlled with sufficient repetition to help memorising, but there should not be unnatural repetition. The repetition should be in different contexts.

Is the series well-graded? The steps between one book and the next should be gradual. Frequently there are 'jumps' and gaps are created. These gaps have to be filled with appropriate books from other schemes. The first books should not be too long and offer relatively quick success in order to give further encouragement. It is useful if the scheme includes activities and games.

Books should have brightly coloured covers and they should be durable and well-bound. The illustrations should be good and helpful to the reading of the text. They should preferably be realistic with no distortions. The print should be good, large and clear, especially for the first books, with not too many words on each page. Is there consistency in letter shapes? Are the letters consistent with the way the children are writing them? This particularly applies to the letters 'a', 'g' and 'y'.

Does the scheme contain a framework for teaching phonics?

Are the books boy-biased or girl-biased? Girls usually accept boys' books, but boys never accept girls' books.

Assessing Reading Failure

Because the nature of reading ability is very complex, it is only very rarely that reading difficulties can be attributed to a single factor. Usually it is a question of a whole complex of factors which can be regarded as being simultaneously connected with reading difficulties, though the degree of the relationship may vary.

The assessment of a child's reading failure must include a study of his overall physical and psychological development and the possible effects of many factors such as low intelligence, emotional and personality problems, poor language development, physical defects, poor home background, absenteeism and poor school conditions.

Intelligence

Generally speaking, the correlation between success in reading and the intelligence quotient is fairly high. When learning to read, children with low intelligence have a slower pace. I have found that when children with I.Q.'s between 60 and 70 are learning new words they require three times as many repetitions to master these words as children with I.Q.'s between 120 and 130. *But*, I must emphasise that there is a danger that if we attribute reading failure to low intelligence as the basic cause, some teachers may label children as dull because they are poor readers. We must remember that many children of normal intelligence are retarded in reading.

Vocabulary

Is the child able to express himself in sentence form? Does he suffer from a speech defect?

You can test the child's vocabulary by using one of several published vocabulary tests, e.g. *Crichton Vocabulary Scale* for children ten years or below (H. K. Lewis & Co., London), *The English Picture Vocabulary Test* (N.F.E.R.), and other tests in Watts' *Language and Mental Development of Children* (Harrap).

Visual and Auditory Abilities
Assess the following abilities:

1. *visual perception* – the ability to be aware of an image;
2. *visual discrimination* – the ability to appreciate differences and similarities in shape, size and colour;
3. *visual memory* – the ability to recall a visual image;
4. *left/right orientation* – the ability to read a line of print from left to right;
5. *auditory perception* – the ability to be aware of sounds;
6. *auditory discrimination* – the ability to appreciate differences and similarities in sounds;
7. *auditory memory* – the ability to remember a sound which has previously been perceived.

The following tests may be used for assessing the above abilities:

1. Daniels and Diack's *Standard Reading Tests* (Chatto & Windus). This is a battery of tests consisting of both attainment and diagnostic tests.
   Test 2 Copying Abstract Figures
        3 Copying a Sentence
        4 Visual Discrimination and Orientation
        5 Letter Recognition
        6 Aural Discrimination Test

2. Wepman's *Auditory Discrimination Test* (Language Research Associates, Chicago).

3. Further suggestions for tests and exercises are found in:
   (i) Tansley's *Reading and Remedial Reading* (Routledge & Kegan Paul).
   (ii) Moyle's *The Teaching of Reading* (Ward Lock Educational).
   (iii) Hughes' *Aids to Reading* (Evans Bros).

(iv) Jones' *From Left to Right* (Autobates Learning System Ltd.).

Phonic Ability

Is the child able to:

1. appreciate rhyme?
2. discriminate letter sounds?
3. blend sounds?
4. associate a particular sound with a particular letter?

Tests of phonic readiness and further suggestions are found in:

1. Tansley's *Reading and Remedial Reading*.
2. Hughes & Presland's 'Applied Psychology and Backward Readers', Supplement in *Journal and News Letter* Vol. 2 No. 4, Association of Educational Psychologists.

Reading Tests

1. *Word Recognition Tests*

   Burt's *Graded Word Reading Test* (U.L.P.), R.A. 4–15 years.
   Schonell's *Graded Word Reading Test* (Oliver & Boyd), R.A. 5–15 years.
   Vernon's *Graded Word Reading Test* (U.L.P.), R.A. 5–18 years.

These are individual tests and they test the child's ability to recognise a word without the aid of contextual clues. The reading age is found as follows:

$$\frac{\text{No. of words read correctly}}{10} + 5 \text{ years} \quad \cdots\cdots\cdots = \text{R.A.}$$
$$(4 \text{ years for Burt's})$$

2. *Sentence and Prose Reading Tests*

   Watts' *Holborn Reading Scale* (Harrap), R.A. 6–14 years.

Daniels & Diack's *Standard Reading Test 1* (Chatto & Windus), R.A. 5:2–9 years.
Neale's *Analysis of Reading Ability* (Macmillan), R.A. 6–14 years.

If teachers wish to use a reading test which is closer to the natural reading situation then the *Holborn Reading Scale*, consisting of thirty-three sentences, is suitable.

The Standard Reading Test 1 consists of thirty-six questions containing words that increase in difficulty, phonic-wise.

The Neale Analysis of Reading Ability consists of short stories increasing in difficulty. Each story has a full page illustration. This test not only calculates an age for reading accuracy, but also speed of reading and comprehension. A form is used with the test for recording responses and this serves as a useful diagnostic record.

3. *Group Reading Tests*

Spooner's *Group Reading Assessment* (U.L.P.), R.A. 6: 3–11: 7.
Watts' *Sentence Reading Test 1* (N.F.E.R.), R.A. $7\frac{1}{2}$–11: 1.
Southgate's *Group Reading Tests V* (U.L.P.).
Word Selection Test 1, R.A. 5: 9–7: 9.
Sentence Completion Test 2, R.A. 7–9: 7.

Group Reading Tests are useful when a reading survey is required. They are useful if one wishes to isolate those children with well above average and well below average reading attainments. They do not take up as much time as the individual tests. It must be remembered that a child cannot be studied in as much detail as one can using individual tests. One cannot expect an accurate assessment and they are not so helpful diagnostically.

Spooner's test is in three sections and consists mainly of word recognition and comprehension. The first section takes about fifteen minutes. The teacher reads out a word and the children are told to underline this word from a group of five words on the test.

The second part takes about ten minutes and consists of sentence completion exercises.

The third part takes about ten minutes. The teacher reads out a word and the children have to find a word or words from a group which sounds exactly the same.

Watts' test is also useful for a reading survey. The scores obtained result from word recognition and comprehension. This is a sentence completion test.

Southgate's Test 1 assesses word recognition whereas *Test 2* contains a certain amount of comprehension. Each test takes about twenty minutes.

A very useful book is *The Teacher's Guide to Tests and Testing* by S. Jackson (Longman).

References

Baldwin, G., *Patterns of Sound*, Chartwell Press, London, 1969.

Bereiter, C. and **Englemann, S.,** *Teaching Disadvantaged Children in the Pre-School*, Prentice-Hall, N.J., 1966.

Bleasdale, E. and **W.,** *Reading by Rainbow*, Moor Platt Press, Bolton.

Bruce, D. J., 'The analysis of word sounds by young children', *Brit. J. Educ. Psychol.*, **34**, 2, 158–169, 1964.

Buchanan, C. D., *Programmed Reading* (Sullivan Associates), obtainable from McGraw-Hill, London.

Daniels, J. C. and **Diack, H.**, *The Standard Reading Tests*, Chatto & Windus, London, 1958.

Daniels, J. C. and **Diack, H.**, *The Royal Road Readers*, Chatto & Windus, London, 1960.

Diack, H., *Reading and the Psychology of Perception*, Roy Palmer, Nottingham, 1961.

Diack, H., *In Spite of the Alphabet*, Chatto & Windus, London, 1965.

Diack, H., *'Jeff and Liz'. First Stage Reading*, Rank-REC, London, 1969.

Doman, G., *Teach Your Baby to Read*, Jonathan Cape, London, 1963.

Downing, J. A., 'Is a "Mental Age of Six" essential for reading readiness?' *Educ. Res.*, **6**, 16–28, 1963.

Dunn, L. and **Smith, O.**, *The Peabody Language Development Kits*, American Guidance Services, Minneapolis, Minn., 1967.

Fernald, G. M., *Remedial Techniques in Basic School Subjects*, McGraw-Hill, New York, 1943.

Fries, C. C., *Linguistics and Reading*, Holt, Rinehart & Winston, New York, 1966.

Fry, E., 'The diacritical marking system and a preliminary comparison with i.t.a.', in Downing, J. and Brown A. L., *The Second International Reading Symposium*, Cassell, 1967.

Gardner, K., *'Jeff and Liz'. Second Stage Reading*, Rank-REC, London, 1969.

Gattegno, C., *Words in Colour*, Educational Explorers, London, 1962.

Goodacre, E. J., *Teaching Beginners to Read: Report No. 2. Teachers and their Pupils' Home Background*, N.F.E.R., London, 1967.

Gulliford, R., *Backwardness and Educational Failure*, N.F.E.R., London, 1969.

Hughes, J. M., 'Look, hear and say', *Forward Trends*, **10**, 1, 29–32, 1966.

Hughes, J. M., 'Taped lessons to aid teaching of reading', *Teacher in Wales*, **8**, 16, 1–2, 1968. **8**, 17, 15–16, 1968.

Hughes, J. M., 'Learning to read with the tape recorder', *Times Educational Supplement*, 23 May, 1969.

Hughes, J. M., 'The tape recorder as a reading aid', *Teachers World*, 15 August, 1969.

Hughes, J. M., *Aids to Reading*, Evans, 1970.

Hughes, J. M. and **Presland, J. L.**, 'Applied psychology and backward readers', Supplement: *Journal and News Letter*, Association of Educational Psychologists, 1969.

Jackson, S., *A Teacher's Guide to Tests*, Longman.

Jones, J. K., *Colour Story Reading*, Nelson, London, 1967.

Kellmer-Pringle, M. L. et al., *11,000 Seven-Year-Olds*, Longman, London, 1966.

Lewis, M. M., *Language and the Child*, N.F.E.R., London, 1969.

Lynn, R., 'Reading Readiness 11 – Reading readiness and the perceptual abilities of young children', *Educ. Res.*, **6**, 10–15, 1963.

Morris, J. M., *Standards and Progress in Reading*, N.F.E.R., London, 1966.

Mosely, D., *The English Colour Code Programmed Reading Course*, N.S.M.H.C.

Moxon, C. A. V., *A Remedial Reading Method*, Methuen, London, 1962.

Reis, R., *Fun with Phonics*, Cambridge Art Publishers, 1962.

Reports on Education, No. 64, 'Learning to Read', D.E.S., July, 1970.

Roberts, G. R., 'Criteria for an early reading programme', in *Reading Skills: Theory and Practice*, U.K.R.A., Ward Lock Educational, 1970.

Roberts, G. R., *Reading in Primary Schools*, Routledge & Kegan Paul, 1969.

Stern, C. and **Gould, T. S.**, *Children Discover Reading*, Harrap, London, 1966.

Stott, D. H., *The Programmed Reading Kit*, Holmes-McDougall, Edinburgh.

Stott, D. H., *Manual for the Programmed Reading Kit*, Holmes-McDougall, Edinburgh, 1962.

Southgate, V., 'The importance of structure in beginning reading', in *Reading Skills: Theory and Practice*, U.K.R.A., Ward Lock Educational, 1970.

Southgate, V. and **Roberts, G. R.**, *Reading – Which Approach?* U.L.P., 1970.

Tansley, A. E., *Reading and Remedial Reading*, Routledge & Kegan Paul, 1967.

Thackray, D. V., 'The relationship between reading readiness and reading progress', *Brit. J. Educ. Psychol.*, **35**, 252–254, 1965.

Vernon, M. D., 'The investigation of reading problems today', *Brit. J. Educ. Psychol.*, **30**, 2, 146–154, 1960.

Wepman, J., *Auditory Discrimination Test*, Language Research Associates, 1958.

Williams, J. D., 'Some problems involved in the experimental comparison of teaching methods', *Educ. Res.*, **8**, 26–41, 1965.

Index